THE AMBIGUITIES OF DESISTANCE

Praise for *The Ambiguities of Desistance*

David Honeywell's book provides a uniquely critical and reflective exploration of desistance which is both experientially grounded and research-informed. Written in a direct, engaging and challenging style, it deserves to be widely read by scholars, students and practitioners – indeed by anyone and everyone concerned both with supporting desistance from crime and with changing how we do justice. This book is full of voices we need to hear and heed, not least the author's.

–**Professor Fergus McNeill**, *University of Glasgow*

Desistance theory has always benefitted from both the autobiographical perspectives of former prisoners as well as systematic academic study, yet in this fascinating new work, David Honeywell combines both of these sources of expertise, drawing on his own lived experience and rigorous research. The intersection of the two makes for a challenging, original and groundbreaking work and a model for keeping criminological research relevant and vibrant.

–**Professor Shadd Maruna**, *Queen's University Belfast*

In one of the finest books ever written about imprisonment, Men in Prison, Victor Serge declares 'A victory over jail is a great victory'. In this book David Honeywell follows Serge to present his own personal victory and those of others who have emerged from imprisonment and made their way through a university education. These remarkable journeys from institutions at the base of society to those nearer its top are gathered as evidence of the complications of desistance. Dr Honeywell offers the reader rare insights drawn from his own incarceration and his subsequent contributions to convict criminology. Like Serge, Honeywell takes his own prison experience and combines it with others into a particularly vivid and triumphant account of lives that prison did not destroy. Share his victory and theirs when you read this book.

–**Dr Rod Earl**, *The Open University*

THE AMBIGUITIES OF DESISTANCE

Ex-offenders, Higher Education and the Desistance Journey

BY

DAVID HONEYWELL

University of Manchester, UK

emerald
PUBLISHING

United Kingdom – North America – Japan – India
Malaysia – China

Emerald Publishing Limited
Howard House, Wagon Lane, Bingley BD16 1WA, UK

First edition 2021

British Library Cataloguing in Publication Data
A catalogue record for this book is available from the British Library

ISBN: 978-1-83982-787-7 (Print)
ISBN: 978-1-83982-786-0 (Online)
ISBN: 978-1-83982-788-4 (Epub)

CONTENTS

ABOUT THE AUTHOR

Dr David Honeywell is a Research Assistant in the *Division of Psychology and Mental Health*, in the University of Manchester, UK. His current research involves working with suicidal prisoners. He also has a background as a criminology lecturer and has worked at Universities of York, Durham and Hull where he has taught crime and deviance, criminal justice and prisons and desistance. As a convict criminologist, he draws on a unique blend of sociological academic qualifications and his lived experience as a former offender and prisoner to identify, analyse and understand the complexities of desistance from crime and challenges prisoners and ex-prisoners may experience.

PARTICIPANT BIOGRAPHIES

In this section I have included the 'Participants' Biographies, including their demographics such as class, race, gender and sexuality which the participants were asked to identify themselves.

- Carla, 22, was a white, English, middle class, lesbian female. She was sentenced to 18 months' imprisonment for perverting the course of justice (i.e., making a false rape allegation). She also had substance and alcohol abuse issues and also struggled with her own identity as a lesbian woman. She found prison liberating as she was able for the first time in her life explore and express her sexuality with other women. She now works with a major charity that helps other individuals who are experiencing the same issues.
- Charlie, 40, was a white, English, middle class, heterosexual male. He was sentenced to three years' imprisonment for wounding with intent to cause grievous bodily harm. He has struggled to acknowledge his offence and feels shame and guilt over it. He comes from a tightly knit and supportive family which has helped him to rebuild his life. Charlie had gained a degree in criminology before he offended which was related to his work with probation. Prison gave him a new and more positive perspective of his clients. He is now working towards a doctorate.
- Chloe, 38, was a white, English, middle class, heterosexual female. She was sentenced to six years in prison but did not want to disclose any details of why she was imprisoned because of the traumatic memories it invokes. At the time of writing she worked for a prison reform charity but has since moved jobs. She has been successful in higher education gaining both undergraduate and postgraduate degrees.
- Clarissa, 41, was a white, English, working class, heterosexual female. She was in custody 11 times for offences ranging from shop lifting and possession to driving while being disqualified. She has continued to work for the council and has enjoyed delivering guest talks to college students about her previous struggle with substance abuse. Clarissa was a victim of child sexual abuse and later developed drug issues. Education provided her with

opportunities not least, including accommodation where she was able to escape a volatile relationship.

- Dafydd, 27, was a white, Welsh, middle class, heterosexual male. He was sentenced to 14 months' imprisonment and was handed a 4-year driving ban for dangerous driving. He came from a stable middle class background but as a youth had begun truanting with other school friends which was the start of his offending. He arrived at a D Category prison almost immediately after being convicted. Dafydd immediately experienced a privileged prisoner status because of his previous academic achievements and because he had been a full-time university student at the time of his arrest.
- Debbie, 42, was a white, English, working class, heterosexual female. She was sentenced to 18 months in prison for theft from her employer. Education enabled Debbie to transform her life where she has now become an entrusted and successful employee working with ex-offenders, homeless and substance users.
- Dylan, 27, was a white, English, working class, heterosexual male. He served a 15-month prison sentence for violence. He came from a family who were involved in criminality and he had a difficult start at university after disclosing his past during a seminar. He eventually graduated with a degree in criminology and has continued to postgraduate study. Dylan has had to struggle against his past and present barriers, but as this study has demonstrated, he has shown resilience which was developed from education and overcoming hardships.
- Gemma, 34, was a white, English, working class, heterosexual female. She served five prison sentences over her lifetime for drug-related offences. At the time of my study, she was working with individuals with substance abuse issues. Despite her obvious transformation, she has experienced continual stigma and discrimination from the area where she grew up and is well known for her former offending. She began a Leadership and Management degree but only completed part of it as she gained employment.
- Germaine, 29, was a white, English, working class, heterosexual female. She was sentenced to 12 months' imprisonment for drugs offences. She was a high-profile case because of the severity of criminal activities of her family, which made it difficult for her to hide her past. Germaine is interested in fashion and design which led to her gaining a degree. She has financial struggles which at the time of the interview were preventing her continuing on to postgraduate study.
- Gerry, 36, was a white, English, working class, heterosexual male. He served several prison sentences for theft, burglary and street crime. He was

what traditional sociologists would have described as a typical recidivist who continued to re-offend, deliberately choosing deviant behaviour [which included drug dealing] over legitimate means. But although there were predictors and causality of his offending, eventually, he decided to stop. He has since worked for the council and has been successful with continual employment.

- Jimmy, 47, was a white, Scottish, working class, heterosexual male. He served four prison sentences, the last being for five years. He admittedly has never fully desisted but no longer commits acts of violence. He became a teetotaller many years ago as this was his main offending trigger. He has now succeeded in gaining a degree in design and continues to find new projects and enjoys being dad to his small boy.
- Ju Ju, 67, was a white, English, middle class heterosexual male. He was sentenced to seven years and six months for statutory rape. He was British born but has resided in New Zealand most of his life. He was the oldest of the sample and has enjoyed a lifetime career as a psychologist and researcher. Education has been an important part of his life before and after prison which has enabled him to immediately overcome the barriers that others have encountered during their entry into university.
- Judy, 41, was a white, English, middle class, heterosexual female. She had spent time remanded in custody, had served a three-month prison sentence and had spent time on probation for shop lifting. Since Judy was interviewed, she has moved jobs but made her career that helps others from going along the same path as herself. This redemptive approach was distinctive for many of the others also and a main theme within this study.
- Len, 48, was a white, English, working class, heterosexual male. He served a life sentence for murder and continues to deal with the psychological problems that led to his offence. Len has had many internal issues to deal with and even felt education was more of a curse as it opened his eyes to the cruel world he once inhabited. Education, however, still gives him a goal to succeed and he continues his education which he feels has given him structure.
- Melody, 44, was a white, English, working class, heterosexual female. She served a four year prison sentence for violence and fraud. She discovered she had been adopted around the age of six and relates this to her deviance. However, it would seem that it is socially linked but the important

point is that for Melody this link to her birth family gives her sense of identity.

- Peter, 58, was a white, English, middle class, heterosexual male. He was sentenced to three months in the 1980s for incitement to commit arson. He came from a privileged background and had a very good early education. Peter did not have an ongoing criminal lifestyle and therefore felt somewhat unrepresentative for this study. Although during his early years he was sent to prison, this was more of a mere glitch during his more rebellious teens. He has continued to become successful in academe and contributes widely to criminological research.
- Ruby, 40, was a white, English, working class, heterosexual female. She served several short-term prison sentences for shop lifting, assault and drug use. She has worked with other individuals with substance abuse issues and is now a trainee probation officer. It was essential for Ruby to demonstrate her independence and gain a degree in criminology and sustain successful employment.
- Sid, 47, was a white, English, working class, heterosexual male. He was sentenced to three years' imprisonment for drug dealing. He is a university lecturer and a convict criminologist who gained a degree in criminology and continued his education to doctoral level. Sid is active in prisoner and desistance research and has been instrumental in networking and mentoring of other individuals who have left prison.
- Stacey, 26, was a white, English, middle class, heterosexual female and one of the youngest of the sample. She had the longest criminal record than the others with over 100 convictions which included mainly violence and criminal damage. Her background gives a fascinating insight into the pains of teenage angst, living in care and decline into criminality. Education was her catalyst for change which was influenced by her mentors with shared lived experiences.
- Tariq, 28, was an English born Asian, middle class, heterosexual male. He was sentenced to two years' imprisonment for violence and disorder. He was the only ethnic minority in the sample, yet his narrative still provided an interesting insight into some of the cultural differences for desisters. He had good support from his family which is supported by other desistance studies. Tariq was also one of the few who already had a university education before he went to prison. He continues with education and has been involved in local community police initiatives and is now working towards a doctorate.

- Tom, 60, was a white, English, middle class, heterosexual male. He was sentenced to 10 years' imprisonment for repeated sex offences. Since leaving prison, he has made progress in academe which boosted his self-esteem and gave him the confidence to confront his past. And although he has experienced more restrictions than anyone else due to the nature of his offences, he feels that higher education enabled a complete transformation of self.

ACKNOWLEDGEMENTS

I would like to thank my mother for all the support she has given over the years. Without her continual belief in me and refusal to give up on me, my life chances would have been very different. Also thanks to my sister Carol who has shown more courage than I ever have and who supported me throughout the financial struggles of funding my PhD.

My circle of academic friends is widespread, yet the criminology community is quite tightly knit. A special thanks goes to those who have been there for me from the start and also to those who have more recently entered my life and continue to support my ventures. My PhD supervisor Gareth Millington was everything a PhD student could want from a supervisor. His patience, understanding and firm guidance saw me through one of the most difficult periods of my life, but if it was not for his believing in me in the first place, I may never have got it off the ground.

I want to thank my mentor and walking partner Professor Maggie O'Neill who has always been there to offer support and guidance as has Professor Simon Winlow who has become a friend and mentor over the years since teaching me at Teesside University in 2001. I would give a special thank you to my friends in desistance. Andy Aresti, a fellow convict criminologist, introduced me to a new concept called desistance at the very beginning of my career in 2013. I have never looked back and Andy has remained a good friend and academic influence throughout. Professor Fergus McNeill's theories of desistance inspired me to develop my own concepts. Fergus has been a good friend and colleague and has always been close at hand to offer academic and personal support over the years. Shadd Maruna has been an enormous influence with his huge wealth of knowledge and groundbreaking ideas and Dr Adam Calverley whose desistance research inspired me early in my career and who later became a good friend and work colleague I had the pleasure to work with at Hull University.

I would like to say how much I am enjoying working with my current team at the University of Manchester on our project about prisoner suicide called PROSPECT. This research is incredibly important, and I feel very lucky to be part of it. A particular thank you to Dr Dan Pratt who not only believed in me but also has made a huge contribution towards the new era of desistance theory, which Professor Shadd Maruna foresees as being mainly steered by ex-prisoner desisters. Dr Pratt has contributed towards this by enabling someone in my position to be a part of such an important study within such a prestigious university for which I will be eternally grateful.

Finally, I would like to thank all my students past and present who make my job so worthwhile. The continual cohort of students and popularity of criminology not only made my life transition from prison to university possible, but also my students' energy and enthusiasm has always kept me on my toes. I know at times we do not see 'eye to eye' but the unique bond I have always had with my students and their interest in my lived experience as a former prisoner has been heart-warming to say to least.

A final thanks to all those who have unknowingly and knowingly helped me through my desistance journey.

1

INTRODUCING DESISTANCE THROUGH THE LIVED EXPERIENCE

> *Little of what we know about prison comes from the mouths of prisoners, and very few academic accounts of prison life manage to convey some of its most profound and important features: its daily pressures and frustrations, the culture of the wings and landings, and the relationships which shape the everyday experience of being imprisoned.*
>
> *(Crewe and Bennett, 2012: ii)*

BACKGROUND

The Ambiguities of Desistance is based on my PhD thesis, written in 2013–2018 which was about ex-prisoners and their self-transformation through higher education. Education was at the forefront of my study where I interviewed 24 individuals both males and females with three broad research questions: (1) How does the reformed ex-prisoner experience self-change and negotiate his/her ex-offender status through education? (2) What impact does higher education have on the ex-offender in terms of rehabilitation? (3) What barriers constrain the ex-prisoner's transition into conventional society, and in particular his/her chosen career path? Initially I set out to prove how transformative education was for ex-prisoners but it soon became clear that the complexities of their stories were worthy of a desistance focussed analysis.

WHAT IS DESISTANCE?

Desistance is taken from the term 'desist' which means to abstain from doing something. There are many examples of desisting from something but criminologists have used its meaning to coin the term 'desistance' (abstaining from crime). And scholars of this theory tend to favour it as having a process that includes a beginning (a willingness to change), a middle (identity transformation) and an end goal (reintegration and acceptance). I argue that desistance in many cases is much more chaotic than this and is much less to do with abstaining from crime and criminal activity. It is more about making significant lifestyle changes and choices and thus desistance is in fact an ongoing and never-ending process. This is supported by desistance studies associated with drug users and the notion of the 'chicken and egg' factor (see Colman and Vander Laenen, 2012). Colman and Vander Laenen posit that while desistance often focuses predominantly on why and how offenders move away from crime, it is often the case that the secondary factor (identity transformation) and recovery from such as substance abuse needs to be addressed first.

Albertson et al. (2015) also found that amongst military veteran desisters, recovery from drug use involved a whole set of social interactions and transitions. This is supported by Best et al. (2008) who found that abstinence was sustained by social network factors (moving away from drug-using friends and support from non-using friends) and practical factors such as accommodation and employment as well as religious or spiritual factors (p. 619).

These findings are unsurprising which is a common theme within desistance studies that often show what you might expect. It seems completely obvious that if someone has a stable home and a job and is accepted within society, they are more likely to be well-rounded citizens. Therefore, stability would clearly give someone more chance of transforming their lives than if they remained in the same chaos from where their problems arose. If we take the environment, for example, some of my interviewees who had battled drug use and domestic violence were able to completely change their lives by moving into their university halls of residence.

It has taken many years of analysis but most desistance scholars now tend to stress that desistance includes the interplay between ageing, informal social control and cognitive transformation theories. But it is not just about getting older, getting married or getting a job, but what significance these things all have and how stabilising they are. Getting older may bring more isolation and less employment opportunities. A job might be highly stressful for some individuals and not be suitable for their temperament or it might not pay enough. A marriage may be toxic and exacerbate further offending, so while desistance theories point to these things as contributing towards change, it merely scratches the surface.

One thing that can be agreed by all is that there has to be an initial decision to give up crime (Cusson and Pinsonneault, 1986). Cusson and Pinsonneault (1986) argue that rational choice (see also Cornish and Clarke, 1986) usually stems from shock such as being wounded in a bank robbery; growing tired of prison; anxieties related to crime; and taking stock of what is most important to them. This may be true, but they will only change when they want to change because whatever the catalyst to change might be, desistance is a subjective choice. And even the most serious criminals can and often do eventually decide to make changes in their lives and abstain from crime.

Earlier desistance studies focussed on external factors being the most influential on self-change using an informal social control perspective which discussed 'turning points' such as marriage, college, employment and the military as being influential on reform (Laub and Sampson, 2003; Shover, 1996). Sampson and Laub's (1993) informal social control theory was a follow-up of Glueck and Glueck's (1940) earlier work which argued that ageing was the only factor which emerged as significant in the reformative processes. But although 'age remains among the best predictors of desistance' (as cited in McNeill et al., 2012, p. 4), this theory is not without its flaws because the ageing process can occur in ways other than biologically, such as through maturation excelled through life experiences (Rutter, 1996).

SO WHEN IS SOMEONE A FULLY FLEDGED DESISTER?

More recently, there has been more focus on subjective transformations (Burnett and Maruna, 2004; LeBel et al., 2008; Maruna, 2001). Examples of this come from Giordano et al. (2002) and Farrall (2005) who argue that would-be desisters need to identify a 'blue print' for the 'sort of' person they want to become which is partly about role-adoption and partly about identifying a set of values or moral standards. Maruna (2001) extends this notion by examining how desisters use a method of re-biographing where desisters reinterpret their past in such away as to recast their past experiences as needing to have occurred for the 'real me' to emerge. They display an 'almost missionary sense of purpose in life' (Maruna, 2001, p. 9) and construct new narratives of their past in order to make sense of the past and the future. In other words desisters see their past experiences as having been essential in making them the better person they are today.

That is not to say that they do not still feel shame and regret for their previous activities which is something that Farrall and Calverley (2006) suggest are most common towards the end of the emotional trajectory. This emotional trajectory is clearly outlined within Giordano et al.'s (2002) four-part theory of cognitive transformation: (1) A general cognitive openness to change; (2) Exposure and reaction to 'hooks for change' or turning points; (3) The envisioning of an appealing and conventional 'replacement self' and (4) A transformation in the way the actor views deviant behaviour so in other words, the transformative process eventually leads to a less favourable perspective of deviance. Giordano and colleagues extended the cognitive transformation theory through exploring spirituality and desistance which Maruna et al. (2006) also examined in their study of religious conversion. It offers an additional perspective of life transformations whereby individuals find religion as a hook for change (Giordano et al., 2002) and the religious community enables belonging and reintegration (McNeill, 2016). But Giordano et al.'s (2008) study supports the argument that desistance from crime is limited with its focus on crime. They argue, their results were unable to provide lasting changes through an individual's religious faith alone without the influence of other factors such as socio-economic factors that relate to desistance from crime. They suggest further research would benefit from a broader focus on areas of life other than criminality that may be enhanced by a strong religious faith, including mental health and parenting outcomes (as cited in Giordano et al., 2008).

In other words, religious faith did not just impact on moving away from crime but also other aspects of the life transition. Although religion effects can be viewed usefully through the lens of social control, acquiring a spiritual foundation is also compatible with the principles of differential association theory, particularly symbolic interactionist versions (e.g. Giordano et al., 2002; Matsueda and Heimer, 1997). Thus, 'religion can be viewed not only as a source of external control over individual conduct but also as a catalyst for new definitions of the situation and as a cognitive blueprint for how one is to proceed as a changed individual' (as cited in Giordano et al., 2008, p. 102).

Introspection through the narrative approach which Maruna (2001) refers to as, 'within-person' changes are essential for the transformation of self as ex-offenders must continually address their offending 'triggers' and be self-critical of their own identities in order to make that transition. And though both informal social control and subjective approaches are equally important, 'individualisation discourse' puts the onus on the individual offender, thus eradicating the state from any blame (Barry, 2015, p. 94).

This is all very inspiring but the question still remains of when someone can be said (without any shadow of a doubt) to have successfully desisted? Perhaps someone who has desisted from serious criminal activity and has settled into a life with legitimated employment has a habit of breaking the speed limit. On occasions this person may have their licence revoked and even appeared in court but does that mean they have not desisted from crime? Proving one has changed is a continual onus on desisters but there are encouraging changes on the horizon in the United Kingdom as a direct result of a campaign known as 'ban the box' (see Unlock, 2018). 'Ban the box' encourages employers to change their recruitment policies towards people with convictions which has now been mirrored in relation to university admissions policies (see UCAS, 2018; University of Westminster, 2018). Not all organisations and universities are as on board with this as they should be, nevertheless it still offers some hope for those whose past demeanors continually blight their futures. Without hope, it is easier for many to revert back to their old ways and Burnett and Maruna (2004) identify hope as an important emotion in desires to desist. This was supported by Farrall and Calverley's (2006) study of emotional trajectories of desistance (i.e. the shifting emotions experienced during processes of desistance). Initially, hopes are for a 'better life' and sustain motivations to desist, whereas later, hopes become more concrete and more closely related to 'conventional' aspirations (better job, larger house, etc). But how does one maintain hope when they are being constantly defined by their worst life mistakes? It is agreed that desistance includes a transformative process which involves a reconstruction of new identities (Maruna, 2001) and reintegration, but the literature falls short of examining the ongoing complex challenges within long-term desistance (McNeill, 2016).

McNeill's tertiary desistance notion offers an important additional stage of the process, whereby individuals become part of a conventional community. This not only includes shifts in behaviours and identities but also shifts in one's sense of belonging to a (moral) community. It extends Maruna and Farrall's (2004) primary and secondary desistance concept which involve lulls (see Weaver and McNeill, 2007) in and out of criminal activity which eventually subside as they progress towards developing new identities. The tertiary stage adds to this by including how desisters reintegrate within conventional society which posits that since identity is socially constructed and negotiated, securing long-term change depends not just on how one sees oneself but also on how one is seen by others.

This suggests that external factors are still significant and essential contributors to successful desistance but not as a whole. That said, what is successful desistance anyway? Is it when someone has not offended for five years?

10 years? because unless it can be determined that someone never re-offended by the time they die, how can anyone measure or determine the completed cycle of desistance? Perhaps the answer can only come from within? The problem here of course is whether the desister would be believed.

DESISTANCE VERSUS REHABILITATION

There are systemic failures where authorities are only interested in how desistance can reduce re-offending which fails to address the more subjective, intuitive and emotional aspects of the desistance journey. Weaver and McNeill (2007) argue that it takes time to change entrenched behaviours and the problems that underlie them and therefore the criminal justice system should expect it to be a zig-zag process (Weaver and McNeill, 2007; Bilby et al., 2013) and therefore be more sparing with imprisonment. This is because of the complexities of the desistance journey and by using prison every time a desister relapses merely delays the desistance process for many more years.

At least with the recent emergence of desistance theory the self-determination and honest attempts to change by many people with criminal convictions is now validated within academic literature. The outdated notion of rehabilitation suggests someone needs fixing and that change has to be forced upon individuals, but as desistance scholars have demonstrated, self-change can only occur by one's own volition:

> *The study of desistance, in fact, originally emerged out of something of a critique of the professionally driven 'medical model' of rehabilitation. To explore desistance (sometimes referred to as 'spontaneous desistance' in early writing, drawing on the notion of 'spontaneous remission' in medicine) was to study those persons who change without the assistance of correctional interventions. From such a perspective, one either 'desists' on one's own accord or else one is 'rehabilitated' through formal counselling or 'treatment'.*
>
> *(Maruna, 2016, p. 292)*

Ward et al. (2012) emphasise an important point which is that psychologists use the term 'rehabilitation', while criminologists are understandably suspicious of its implication that individuals are being returned to a more acceptable set of behaviours. It is evident that the distinction between rehabilitation and desistance is still not fully understood by most. The process of desistance has been around for a long time, it is just that people tend to claim individuals have been rehabilitated when they have actually desisted. Rehabilitation has always been the favoured narrative because it suggests someone has been forced to change or see the errors of their ways. This fits with the societal expectations and the collective consciousness of social construct rather than accepting people can and do change themselves.

This is why I feel education has always been appealing to prisoners because of how one finds education and makes a personal decision to embark on a programme of self-change and discovery. Education enables prisoners self-expression and an ability to develop emotionally, psychologically and intellectually. It is also a personal journey created from one's own volition so this alone positions education firmly within the desistance narrative. This further emphasises my argument in Chapter 2 that education in prison as a process towards early desistance is nothing new. It also leads me back to my earlier argument that a desistance culture within prisons would be a step in the right direction (see McNeill and Schinkel, 2016). We are not exploring some wild and bizarre concept but merely identifying and nurturing something which already exists. Rather than this idea being alien, it is just that we have only recently developed a theory called desistance.

EXAMINING THE DESISTANCE NARRATIVE

Moving away from crime and criminality should not always be the main focus which has always been the case within mainstream criminology but something narrative criminology continues to rectify. Even classic sociology and criminology studies such as the Chicago School in the 1930s (e.g. Shaw, 1931; Landesco, 1933; Sutherland, 1937) and desistance studies in the 1990s which have included autobiographical accounts that have not been widely acknowledged much within mainstream criminology (Presser and Sandberg, 2015). Yet Sykes and Matza's (1957) neutralisation theory of how offenders play down their offences has stood the test of time and is still very much used in theoretical criminology teaching. This could be because of its emphasis on offenders being homogeneous and that they will always try to justify their actions. However, it could be argued that playing down one's own offending could in some instances be associated to feelings of shame and low self-esteem. Also, a completely unexplored area within narrative criminology is how some ex-offenders over-disclose their pasts to sometimes complete strangers. Is this a way of making sense of their lives and excusing oneself? It could be a way of re-negotiating identities (i.e. trying to make sense of the world and re-biographing) (Maruna, 2001) or even a way of apologising. To put this into further context of neutralisation narratives, over-disclosing could be a way of dissociating oneself from past offending followed by reconstructive narrative (Maruna, 2001). For example, following a six-year prison sentence, 38-year-old Chloe explains:

> *I just felt like, I'd tell everybody because, I felt like everybody knew, like it was stamped on me and I would literally tell people [upset] probably inappropriately, over disclosing.*
>
> *(Chloe)*

This is something I can personally relate to but have never seen discussed in any literature and it is these types of nuances of the desistance narrative I wish to further explore within and beyond this book. My personal experience and the process and subsequent immersion in the theory are an original and ground-breaking feature of this book. It is also very timely as it resonates with Shadd Maruna's (2017) *Desistance as a Social Movement* prediction that the new era of desistance stories will come from ex-prisoner desisters themselves. The Convict Criminologist Organisation has already made significant leaps in this regard through a combination of first-hand experiences of the criminal justice system within academic research. There are many ex-prisoner activists and ex-prisoner scholars, some of whose interviews are used in this book, but as far as I am aware, there is no other desistance scholarship written by ex-prisoner desisters other than myself and fellow convict criminologist, Andy Aresti (see Aresti et al., 2010).

CHAPTER SUMMARY

There are four key chapters within this book which focus on the key desistance themes I have already outlined. In Chapter 2, building on the work of McNeill and Schinkel (2016) I will discuss how prisons may adopt a desistance model as part of their culture and draw on the narratives of those who claim prison provided time and space to make positive life changes. Susie Scott's theory of 'reinventive institutions' led me to develop an argument about how ambiguous institutions have become in recent years. Universities which are supposed to be liberal and inclusive of diverse groups are being punitive towards people with convictions. On the other hand, we are seeing more prison governors adopting a transformative approach towards prisoner education, thus furthering the ambiguity of institutions which I explore in the section *Institutional ambiguities and the rise of desistance consumers*. Following the institutional theme, I begin to develop my argument of why desistance is never-ending by building on Nugent and Schinkel's 'pains of desistance' (2016). A parallel of Syke's 'pains of imprisonment' Nugent and Schinkel rightly argue that desistance is often a painful experience which includes feelings of isolation.

This can be extended using Healy's (2010, 2014) 'liminal desistance' or 'liminality' (where individuals often remain within an existence of stagnation) thus forcing desistance to be continuous. Equally, painful desistance experiences can be used as positive experiences – an idea which I examine through the lens of Maruna's (2001) 'redemptive script'. I argue that revisiting traumatic memories is an important method of cultivating a new sense of self. This makes desistance an ongoing journey, but as a necessary consequence and one that has been successfully cultivated by 'convict criminologists' and those who use their lived experiences for generative roles as counsellors and mentors.

Narrative criminology is central to this book and recurs in every chapter as the importance of discourse is emphasised, but here, I merge my notion of 'the painful narrative' with the pains of desistance. But rather than discussing the negativity of painful desistance experiences, I discuss the importance of revisiting past traumatic events which are mostly associated with abuse, drugs, homelessness and imprisonment, but for one individual, education itself was traumatic. He recalls how studying sociology and criminology opened doorways to his mind he felt was like a curse. Learning about sociological theories revealed how abusive his life really had been which until then he had normalised.

In Chapter 4, I explore the self-stories and narratives of my interviewees and how their stories become essential towards their own self-change and identity transformation but equally how these stories merge with my own experiences. This is an example of 'reflexivity in action' whereby my insider/outsider identity is challenged during and following the interviewing process. This essential aspect of research is often omitted by researchers and more so by those who share the same lived experiences as their participants, despite attempts from the discipline of existential sociology (see Kotarba and Fontana, 1984). And now in my current role as a prison researcher I am poised to enter the prison estate once again but this time with my own identity in tact where I will be interviewing suicidal prisoners. Their stories will mirror my own experiences yet I can only imagine what challenges await me.

We know that the storytelling of past experiences is an important process of self-transformation and we can see evidence of this in relation to the redemptive script. We know that people use their past experiences to make sense of their future selves and that by sharing these stories they are able to make identity transitions. Some of the participants in my PhD study owned their painful experiences of being homeless; physically, mentally, sexually abused; and stigmatised and rejected. And in their roles as counsellors, mentors and teachers, they draw heavily from their most painful experiences to drive forward the messages of hope to others. It is their way of giving back and at the same time self-healing (Maruna, 2001; Frank, 1995).

The controversial branch of criminology 'convict criminology' has an important presence throughout this book, and Chapter 5 draws specifically on the narratives (Vaughan, 2007) of several desisters who self-identify as convict criminologists (ex-prisoners turned academics). The trajectories of convict criminologists challenge the very essence of desistance theories which argue that it is essential to separate one's past and present identities because convict criminologists maintain a dual identity which allows them to forge tenured academic careers (see Ross et al., 2010). But that does not mean that reaching such a privileged pinnacle does not come without many struggles and hardships along the way as Ross and colleagues argue in their paper *Convict criminology and the struggle for inclusion* (2016). Another dynamic is that of the ex-'service user' turned mentor who in contrast to convict criminologists use their past experiences to inform their roles but more covertly. Maruna (2001) refers to these individuals as 'wounded healers' (p. 102) who use their past experiences to work in generative roles to help save others from repeating their own destructive paths.

This notion also resonates with Arthur Frank's (1995) concept of 'the wounded storyteller' which essentially involves a narrative relating to ill health which can be translated to drawing strength from past struggles with mental health issues and substance abuse. The final section of the final chapter focusses on the ultimate vehicle of the interviewees' trajectories which was higher education and the university culture. But rather than focussing on the unsurprisingly positive transformation of education, here I focus on the higher education community as an essential escape for some while others were denied this privilege. Living on university campus was an escape from difficult environments for some while others were denied this chance due to their convictions and therefore remained within the environment from which they were desperate to escape. It also explores the limitation of education for some individuals who remain within a desistance purgatory, while those who already held degrees when they imprisoned were afforded a privileged status within the prison education department where they were somehow held on a pedestal as educated professionals.

2

THE AMBIGUITIES OF INSTITUTIONS

> *It is true that in some cases the recipient does not find the punishment painful, or even welcomes it – for example, some offenders might find prison a refuge against the intolerable pressures of the outside world.*
>
> *(Cavadino et al., 2020,* The Penal System*)*

Few desistance theories have made links to the potential influences imprisonment can have on the early stages of the desistance process or that the influence imprisonment can aid self-change. This is because desistance is focussed on post-release social factors and also because any thoughts of imprisonment influencing positive change go against the idea of what prison is for – which in itself is ambiguous. In actual fact, there are many examples of links between imprisonment and desistance with a recurring finding that some prisoners associate their time in prison with positive self-transformation (see Honeywell, 2018; Schinkel, 2015; McNeill and Schinkel, 2016; McLean et al., 2017; Giordano et al., 2002).

It is important to emphasise here that prison should not be seen as a place where people thrive, which Kazemian (2020) explains in her recent study of French prisoners. In her book, *Positive Growth and Redemption in Prison*, she poses the question of whether individuals can thrive in prison. We are already aware that many people suffer in prison but through the lens of Comfort (2012), Kazemian argues that prisoners do not thrive but rather find change through being forced by the surroundings, time and space. And while the pains of imprisonment clearly exist, it is important to understand that positives can be drawn from these very difficult situations. Kazemian rightly argues that in desistance research, while scholars offer constant reminders that focussing solely on negative outcomes does not capture the full picture, the same applies to the effects of imprisonment. In other words, good and bad experiences should be discussed in relation to desistance and also imprisonment.

PRISONS AND DESISTANCE

The very nature of imprisonment has always been to inflict pain and punishment, a view not only supported by many contemporary writers but also consistently supported by the dated yet still relevant theory of Sykes' (1958) 'pains of imprisonment'. Sykes emphasises five key deprivations that prisoners experience. For example, 'the deprivation of liberty', caused by isolation and over time; the 'deprivation of goods and services' where prisoners do not have the right of ownership; the 'deprivation of heterosexual relationships', which is 'involuntary celibacy'; 'the deprivation of autonomy' where prisoners are denied self-determination or the ability to make choices and the 'deprivation of security' through the infliction of 'prolonged intimacy' with violent and aggressive men (p. 78). Additionally, despite some more modern variations on Sykes' theory to accommodate changing times (Crewe, 2011), his theory is as relevant today as it was over 60 years ago. Therefore, with such a lasting legacy about what is clearly an embedded culture of pain and punishment, the idea of desistance and prison being used interchangeably may seem far fetched to say the least. But if we delve a little deeper, we can see that desistance has been happening in prisons for decades. There are many well-documented 'boy made good' stories that began inside prison but the media hype around these cases was not so focussed on the underpinning desistance themes that were crucial to these individual's transformations.

Largely forgotten today, but two of the most compelling accounts of 'making good' (Maruna, 2001) are that of former London bank robber John McVicar and Glaswegian gangster Jimmy Boyle. McVicar wrote an extensive account of his criminal past and transition through higher education while serving a 23-year prison sentence in the 1970s (McVicar, 1974). McVicar was later propelled from public enemy number one to gaining a first-class honours degree in sociology to becoming a postgraduate and later a journalist. Also, in Cohen and Taylor's (1981) second edition of the *Psychological Survival of*

Long Term Imprisonment, McVicar recounts his participation as 'Chris' in Cohen and Taylor's study and how their sociological teachings in Durham prison, where he was at the time, led to his fascination for the subject.[1] In 2009, Anthropologist Jed Tucker argued that McVicar's example of a transforming life raises important questions about common understandings of educational programmes in prisons and about prisoners' criminal 'master status' (see Becker, 1963). McVicar enrolled in a college programme out of boredom and described his personal change as an 'unintended consequence' of pursuing a degree (in Tucker, 2009, p. 27). Nevertheless, his continual pursuit of education led to a life-changing transformation.

Another similar and equally influential narrative was written by Jimmy Boyle, a Glaswegian born gangster who while in Barlinnie prison in 1976 wrote his life story *A Sense of Freedom* (1977), which has since become a bestseller, a film and 40 years later, reprinted as a classic of prison literature (Campbell, 2016). Furthermore, Boyle became a world-renowned sculptor, a craft he learned during his time in prison. Yet such accounts of compelling transformations by former criminals who at one time were deemed enemies of the State and imprisoned for decades have only just began to surface within academic literature and can now be seen in university reading lists for criminology students.[2]

There are many other examples of similar but less famous stories but I chose these two particular cases because of how much their stories influenced my own trajectory and how their autobiographies helped me think about education as an escape from my dysfunctional and directionless life. There is less attention given to the many individuals around the world who find their hook to change (Giordano et al., 2002) during or after their time in prison and even less attention given to the many 'girl made good' stories. But this book will go some way towards filling that gap. As I have said, links between desistance and prison are unheard of anyway, but it has always been implicit.

At the time I was conducting my PhD study, Debbie was a 42-year-old manager within a charity organisation that supports ex-offenders and others with substance abuse issues and homelessness. Before working in this role she had served 18 months' imprisonment for theft from her previous employer, but her time in prison was more of an escape from her chaotic lifestyle than

1 *Psychological Survival of Long Term Imprisonment* was first published in 1972 and again in 1981.

2 Jimmy Boyle is referred to in the student textbook *Prisons and Punishment: The Essentials* by Scott and Flynn (2014).

punishment. There is no doubt that she suffered as a result of being kept apart from her daughter, but compared to her home life, prison was closer to a respite than a punishment.

Debbie felt that the worst part of being in prison was being separated from her daughter, yet at the same time prison provided her with a more structured life by removing the burdens that were dominating her existence outside. This would benefit her children in the long term because prison provided Debbie with the space she needed to re-evaluate her life which she was later able to transform through education. This has led to her becoming an entrusted and successful employee but her journey towards a better life began while she was in prison. This was Debbie's response when she was asked what being prison was like for her:

> *Do you know, this is awful. I didn't find it [prison] bad. Because I got took away from what I'd done [crime]. So the actual people that were suffering on the outside was my child, my mum, my brother – all good people. All never done anything wrong. Hard working people were left with gossip and I was took away with it. By the time I got out of it, newspaper – chippy wrapping.*
>
> *(Debbie)*

It can be argued that when people commit crime, the impact it may have on their family is the last thing on their mind. Debbie does identify with those she left behind and is able to understand not only how prison affects the loved ones of prisoners but also how she needed this escape to self-reflect.

> *You've got no worries, you've no bills to pay and you're not worrying about the rift. You do worry about your child. That's the bit I miss – is that I was taken away from my child. That was the punishment! That was the worst part of it! I missed Christmas! I missed her birthday!*
>
> *(Debbie)*

Debbie also makes reference to how life became a struggle once she left the structured environment that prison provided.

> *Trying to move on from that is a different story, but I think they had the worst ride than me. I went there [prison] expecting something like 'Bad Girls' [TV women's prison series].*
>
> *(Debbie)*

It is all too often the case that while the structure of prison holds things together, once back outside, a person's life begins to unravel. The benefits of routine and structure within prison are emphasised when one considers that once released many revert to the lifestyle that led them to prison in the first instance. The desistance process was not as pertinent to Debbie's predicament because she was not a persistent offender (Maruna, 2001). Examples such as Debbie's are more about making common lifestyle changes rather than trying to abstain from habitual criminal activities. These are much more relevant to career criminals or those whose lives have included multiple experiences within the criminal justice system. With this in mind, if for people like Debbie, desistance means nothing more than changing lifestyles that led to their imprisonment; this shows how easy it can be for the average person to end up in prison.

Debbie discusses the impact mother and child separation has on women in prison which she emphasises as being her 'real' punishment (Carlen and Worrall, 2004). Prison also provided her with some relief from the everyday domestic worries such as paying the bills and also coercive domestic violence. Each of these cases grapples with a new concept of the total institution and reinventive institutional paradoxes (see Scott, 2015). Prisons are not designed to rehabilitate or assist prisoners to transform their lives but rather to punish, yet some prisoners are finding ways of making prison work for them. This says more about the individuals themselves than the institutions where prisoners are finding new ways of drawing positive experiences from their time of incarceration. This suggests an underexplored resilience (see Scott, 2015) as we saw in Debbie's example which provides a clear message that prisons do not need to be harsh and punishment-focussed to make people go on to become better individuals. What has become clear is that it can merely be the time and space of a prison environment that helps change which triggers early desistance. Therefore, there is an argument for a desistance culture being nurtured within the prison environment (Schinkel, 2015; McNeill and Schinkel, 2016). The notion of a desistance approach in prisons has been addressed by desistance scholars in relation to Scottish prisons (see Schinkel (2015) and McNeill and Schinkel (2016)), but is desistance in prison really anything new? The impact of imprisonment evoking positive self-change has been happening for a long time but completely escaped any major academic studies because the focus on prison research is around punishment and rehabilitation. The common denominator here is the term 'rehabilitation', which I referred to earlier where I discussed the nature of desistance being a self-process of change as opposed to rehabilitation which is a forced attempt by the criminal justice system to change a person. You could argue that prison rehabilitated Debbie by forcing her to re-evaluate her life, but no amount of incarceration will change a person until that person is ready to change. There is no doubt that the exogenous experience of being imprisoned can force change which can trigger the primary stages of desistance where individuals are shocked into rethinking their futures (Cusson and Pinsonneault, 1986). This existential crisis of the self caused by incarceration can sometimes be enough to at least evoke an openness for change and sense of imagined redirection (Giordano et al., 2002).

When 40-year-old Charlie was sent to prison, he was already struggling with some difficult personal issues and, after committing his offence (wounding with intent to cause Grievous Bodily Harm), became ostracised and stigmatised by both his employers and his university. We will come back to Charlie in the following section of institutional ambiguities when we learn of his experiences at university. The following narrative follows what happened leading up to his prison sentence and once he was in prison:

> *I basically stabbed my girlfriend and I had attempted suicide on the three days before it happened. I had a nervous breakdown, I was studying at university and had some very difficult things going on in my life that had resulted in some bizarre behaviour and pressure and things and, yes it wasn't planned.*
>
> *(Charlie)*

Charlie's narrative encapsulates the enormity of how desperate he was feeling that led him to self-harm. Fortunately he later began forging new alliances where he then began to reassess how he views himself.

> *I was a broken man and the fear of custody and what I imagined prison life to be like ... I slashed my wrists. [...] but I had people who looked out for me and who I became friends with and who supported me.*
>
> *(Charlie)*

He began a transition towards his 'core self' or 'real me', which Maruna (2001, p. 131) explains as something distinct from the person who committed crimes in their past; this is a process of re-biographing identities. Therefore, although Charlie's crises continue to cause him inner conflict due to feelings of shame, he begins to develop a network of support and gradually begins to view himself more positively:

> *I got on with well with a lot of the lads in there and the prison staff were supportive, and because I think they realised that something had gone horribly wrong, and I learned, so at times it was horrific but I also gained a lot from prison as well.*
>
> *(Charlie)*

Charlie's probation officer identifies his behaviour as 'not something he does', and through his narrative, he begins to connect with what his probation officer says and disassociate himself from the person who stabbed his girlfriend. At the time of my study, Charlie continued to internalise feelings of guilt and shame because of the severity of his offence and the events that led up to it – a period where he describes himself as a 'broken man'. As I mentioned earlier, in relation to Debbie's story, there is no doubt that desistance 'from crime' was not Charlie's priority because he was not a persistent offender (Maruna, 2001). His core objective of desistance was not abstaining from crime but instead gradually disassociating from his past self. For Debbie, it was a case of making some major lifestyle changes, whereas for Charlie, he had some mental health issues to address. Desistance is a very complex process that incorporates many facets from which individuals can draw upon in order to tailor their specific desistance needs. Desistance is, after all, a self-motivating process, and therefore, desisters are in a position to decide which parts of the process are pertinent to their own needs. Individuals become what I shall refer to as 'desistance consumers', which is especially relevant with education and desistance (see Section Open prisons, education and desistance).

By the very fact they are removed from their chaotic lives outside (as we saw in Debbie's narrative), they are able to find the space and time to make plans and changes. This leads to early desistance and being able to disassociate themselves from the crises associated with their lives outside of prison. This goes some way to arguing a need for prisons to adopt a desistance culture which incorporates a conscious and systemic approach towards nurturing desistance as part of the very fabric of prison life. Imprisonment evoking desistance is nothing really new – what is new is a theory called 'desistance' and the realisation that prison desistance exists. Prisons and desistance have only recently been discussed in academic literature (see McNeill and Schinkel, 2016), yet there are many examples whereby prisoners have used their time constructively not least through education. Education has long been associated with self-change even amongst some of Britain's formerly most wanted criminals of bygone years (see McVicar, 2000;

Boyle, 1977). The biographies and autobiographies of these famous 'boy made good' characters are inspirational to say the least, but the subsequent movies that followed these books only focussed on the violence and brutality of prison life. None ever captured the true essence of the character's eventual transformation through education and how their self-change came about not as a result of some enforced rehabilitation by an institution but through a process of self-searching and being open to the possibility of self-change (see Giordano et al., 2002).

OPEN PRISONS, EDUCATION AND DESISTANCE

As I said earlier, prisons have been actively involved in the process of desistance for decades bit more intentionally within their open estates. This section begins by exploring open prisons in relation to their desistance approaches because there has been little if any empirical research around links between open prisons and desistance since Maguire and Raynor published their paper in 2006: *How the resettlement of prisoners promotes desistance from crime: Or does it?* Prisoners housed in open prisons are able to work in the community, visit family on day release and begin a process of reintegrating, thus strengthening social bonds (Laub and Sampson, 1993). Therefore, open prisons work in contrast to closed prisons by offering measures of freedom and personal responsibility that are denied in closed prisons. However, aspects of the open prison which are barely discussed include hidden controlling factors. Shammas (2015) argues these are uniquely suited to disciplining and controlling prison populations, crucially, by giving inmates something to lose and then threatening to take it away (p. 3). But despite the constant threat of losing one's freedom and easy prison lifestyle, they also represent what all prisons should represent.

Dafydd, 27, was in his second year of a degree when he was sent to prison which made him a person of interest to the prison education department and he immediately experienced a privileged prisoner status. But this favouritism also caused tensions for him with the other prisoners and so he became alienated from his fellow prisoners. Therefore, in a twist to the usual alienation and stigmatisation (stigma) associated within the total institution (Goffman, 1961), Dafydd was being stripped of his identity from his own prison subculture. This usually happens towards those who are convicted of sex offences, but in this case it was because of jealousy. His privileged position landed him with one of the most sought-after jobs in any prison which was in the library, but this attracted the wrong type of attention. According to Dafydd, such a privileged position was in fact usually given to sex offenders which put his safety at risk as well as alienating him from the others:

> *I was tarred with the same brush at first. Most of the camp (open prison) is very segmented. There's different units. They stick to themselves. Even going down for food I sort of couldn't talk to anyone, because I didn't really know them. But I would nod my head and everyone would look at me or just ignore me. You could tell you were being ignored. It was only later when I realised that people had thought that I was the same (sex offender) because I worked in the library.*
>
> *(Dafydd)*

Fortunately, the prison adopted a zero-tolerance policy whereby prisoners were instantly relocated to another prison if they attacked anyone.

> *When I was there one of the boys, one of the sex offenders was in the newspaper for being a sex offender. One of the normal prisoners (non-sex offender), you could say, cut the picture and the clipping out of the paper and stuck it on his door. The next day he was gone.*
>
> *(Dafydd)*

Open prisons are in a very strong position to exercise strict policies because most prisoners want to be in them due to their easy-going regimes and open prisons can be selective. But although open prisons exercise strict control over prisoners with the constant threat of being returned to secure prisons (Shammas, 2015), as the above narrative shows, it is a necessary control for the safety of other prisoners.

> *When I arrived at the 'D' Cat prison, HM Prison, they processed me again and I had an education test. I was Level 3 in both of them. There was an Irish traveller next to me and the woman was asking us what level of education we had. I said I'm in my second year of university and she was very surprised. Whereas, the guy next to me said 'I can't read and write and I don't want to'. That was such a massive contrast.*

We can see from the narrative above the contrasting educational backgrounds between Dafydd who had received a good education and the other prisoner who came from a travelling community, and how they were treated very differently. When asked how entering prison with a university education impacted on him, he said:

> *Oh I think I was looked upon favourably. I think I was looked after you could say [...]. I was moved straight to working in the library. I was also head librarian pretty quick. I had three exams to complete my second year of study [...]. The universities classify it as an overseas examination [...]. The university used to give course work to my girlfriend. She would come down on a visit every Sunday and take the course work that I've done and give me the new course work.*
>
> *(Dafydd)*

There is an important point to raise here about when Dafydd was sent to prison he had already been studying for a degree at university, but unlike Charlie (more on this later), he was allowed to continue his education. This highlights the confusing ambivalence across university policies when dealing with prisoners and education. Dafydd feels that they made an exception with him because they knew him well which is in complete contrast to how other universities had treated other people in my study.

> *I think because they knew me well and not just that, I've been a course representative here (university) for four years. I've always been quite close with the staff and always thought if I get on with someone that's teaching me I learn a lot more.*
>
> *(Dafydd)*

Open prisons are conducive to study because of the more relaxed rules (Aresti and Darke, 2015) which was perhaps why Dafydd was able to get his learning materials brought to the prison. Also, such prisons can have a different impact on the sense of self and are more geared towards adopting a desistance model. This is because prisoners are able to work in the community, take home leaves and be given more responsibility. However, despite the university helping with Dafydd's education, and more privileged conditions that are synonymous of open prisons, some of the prison staff were being deliberately obstructive.

> *I think parts of the prison were accommodating but some of the higher ups in prison don't necessarily agree with the special treatment that some educational prisoners receive. The woman who worked (in the prison) who was the education woman Janice, she was straight away – couldn't do enough to help me*

> *facilitate my studies. The case in point, when I was having my first lot of course work and they sent through the material for study, they wouldn't let it through the first week. He (the prison officer in charge) was adamant, 'No it's not coming in', and that really spoilt my visit.*
>
> *(Dafydd)*

> *DH: Did he give a reason?*
>
> *Dafydd: Because he hadn't had approval or authorisation. Then the following week, because the visits were always on Sunday, that's the only day, we could have visits. So, because of that there was different staff in for the visits and there's no communication with visiting staff you could say and the weekly staff.*

Here we can see another section of those in authority – in this case – working in the criminal justice system being deliberately difficult. Fortunately, Dafydd had the added support of educational staff. Although Dafydd is one of the several of this sample who entered prison with a university education, Dafydd was the only one who managed to continue his course while serving a prison sentence. With encouragement from the prison education staff, Dafydd was able to transform his sense of self through learning and in time he also became integrated amongst his peers. Dafydd was asked if other prisoners used his educational background to help them:

> *The guy I mentioned when I was saying I was doing a degree and he said: 'I can't read and write', he would come into the library and I would read the newspaper to him. He asked me when there was nobody there. He'd come in when we were just about to close. I think he was probably ashamed that he couldn't read and write and he was too proud to ask for help. Whereas he realised that I wasn't going to run around laughing at him and he came out of his shell. I used to sit and read to him.*
>
> *(Dafydd)*

Here we can see the impact of how low educational abilities can impact on the sense of self, but we can also see a sensitive side of prison life that is never mentioned and how some prisoners help one another. This is an interesting insight into a more humanising aspect of prison life when one considers the dehumanising process of the prison process. Before entering higher education,

Sid, 47, was also studying at higher education level when he was sentenced to three years in prison:

> *I was in a settlement unit in Kent. They would let me come over to do my finish off my access course. So, I actually did the access course. I was going to the lectures on a Friday coming up to White City, Shepherds Bush way, every Friday and sitting in f.....g classroom with students finishing off my access course. So, I think, for me the environment in prison was helpful in a sense that there weren't the barriers that people are getting now, that I am hearing about. Stuff could get sent in to the education department [...] my wife was sending in the books, psychology books and stuff.*
>
> *(Sid)*

Sid found his experience of the open prison very rewarding as he was freely able to follow a course of higher education, but as explained earlier, even within the open surroundings, he still felt a crisis of the self which amounted to a state of liminality (see Healy, 2010, 2014). Liminality is something which I shall discuss further along.

> *So, for me I guess I had a clear goal. I knew that when I was in prison, I knew that I was going to do this access course and then going to university. I knew that in my head. I could have f....d that up by going round being tough either so I needed to be careful. So, there was, I wouldn't say tension, but there was this identity of... yeah you've still got to be tough because you're in prison and masculine. But actually, your being a student, and usually the two don't go together, but actually for me they do. It's never been an issue and actually it's quite a novelty as you probably know. I guess what I am trying to say that, when I was a kid, f..k that, the studying, they're all the geeks! I want to get out and get in to trouble and get that thrill but for me they are very compatible – those two identities.*
>
> *(Sid)*

Sid's narrative explains an interesting perspective where two identities collide (Healy, 2010, 2014). Sid claims that it does not cause tension, but we can see within the narrative how he is trying to make sense of what seems to be an identity crisis. Despite Sid being in an open prison which allowed him a certain amount of freedom to attend college, he was still experiencing an inner conflict of the self. He encapsulates this by saying: 'those two identities', which is something I will explore further when I discuss Bourdieu's (2004) concept of the divided self. They exist within a liminal world of imprisonment and freedom where part of their time is spent working or studying within the local community and the rest of their time is spent within the confines of a prison environment.

INSTITUTIONAL AMBIGUITIES AND THE RISE OF 'DESISTANCE CONSUMERS'

Prisons and universities have both created a polarisation from their usual ethos, because prisons are becoming more pro education and universities are becoming more punitive towards people with convictions. But this is not a complete condemnation of universities who are more than ever constrained to adhering to safeguarding rules. Universities all have safeguarding policies which generally are a process of making sure vulnerable children, young people and adults are protected from being abused, neglected or exploited. Therefore, it is understandable that criminal convictions might be important, but there is no evidence at all to suggest anyone with previous convictions has ever been, or is likely to be, a liability. From May 2018, applicants for courses starting in 2019 onwards were no longer required to declare whether they had any relevant 'unspent' criminal convictions when making applications to higher education through the Universities and Colleges Admissions Service (UCAS).[3] Ben Jordan, Senior Policy and Qualifications Manager, said: 'UCAS is committed to ensuring that anyone who wants to study at university or college has the opportunity to apply, and isn't put off by questions on the application'. In previous years, everyone was asked to disclose whether they had any unspent, relevant criminal convictions which have now been removed. This is a step in the right direction, but it also means that there is now a greater onus on universities to adopt their own policies around applicants with criminal convictions (Bourdieu, 2004). It also makes it even more essential for individuals with convictions to shop around. Because of these changes and the nuanced approach by universities towards people with convictions, it is more essential than ever for desisters who wish to enter university to become smart 'desistance consumers'

3 UCAS (Universities and Colleges Admissions Service) is an independent charity providing information, advice and admissions services to inspire and facilitate educational progression.

whereby they shop around for universities which are inclusive towards people with convictions. The desisters who choose higher education as their conduit towards their desistance journey make a financial investment for them and their children's future. Yet they can often find themselves out on a limb through nothing more than not understanding their legal rights as consumers with convictions.

None of the participants in my study found the transition from prison to university particularly smooth and some were even met with hostility from individuals in positions of authority. The paradoxes of both prisons and universities are increasing but perhaps with little scrutiny. Both prisons and univerities have confusing and mixed approaches and attitudes towards people with convictions, education and desistance depending on each particular institution. What was clear from my interviews with the interviewees was that when someone with convictions is considering going to university, it pays to shop around. All students take their time in choosing which university best suits their needs because they are consumers who want to make sure they are getting good value for their money. After all, they are going to be spending three years or more of their lives at university where they will inevitably pay a significant amount of money towards their tuition and living costs. For the student with criminal convictions though, shopping around should also involve choosing a university which has a positive and modern attitude towards individuals with criminal convictions. It was clear throughout the interviews that some universities were more inclusive than others, but then how would a student applicant know this? It is practically impossible, which is why there needs to be more transparency. The UCAS website says that Universities and colleges may only need to know about very specific convictions or restrictions (for example, if they cannot access the Internet), and some may not ask at all. It will be different depending on which university they are applying to and applicants are advised to contact their chosen university or college in the first instance.

In an attempt to try and develop the idea of the desistance consumer, I examined the sociology of universities and prisons through the lens of Professor Susie Scott's (2015) concept of 'reinventive institutions'. This is a reverse concept to that of Goffman's (1961) classic 'total institutions' theory which has four key concepts: (1) the unfolding of the daily round in the same place (and under the same authority); (2) batch living (or being treated as part of an anonymous mass); (3) the rigid timetabling and scheduling of activities and (4) an institutional goal of resocialization. Scott offers an alternative perspective to that of Goffman's which claims an increase of people seeking periods of self-reflection, education and enrichment in pursuit of 'self-improvement' within institutions. Institutions such as universities are 'designed to educate, enrich and develop people's talents or abilities' which provides a nuanced approach to the consumer identity of institutions. However, Scott (2015) does not include prisons in her list of reinventive institutions nor does she critique universities as being total institutions. Therefore, my aim is to fill this gap by developing the notion that while some prisons are reinventive institutions, some universities are total institutions. And thus, Scott's argument provides a lens through which to analyse the changing tide of both prisons and universities. While some universities may be reinventive in some aspects, in terms of dealing with people who have criminal convictions, many fall spectacularly short of being reinventive. Therefore, despite Scott's opposition to Goffman's theory being repressive, its four key features do hold some parallels to universities.

On the other hand, while prisons are generally associated with violence and toxic masculinity, some are developing a more creative and nuanced reinventive ethos towards higher education (see Honeywell, 2018; see also Crewe and Levins, 2019). This can be seen with the development of prison to college collaborations (see Durham University, 2014 and Cambridge University, 2016) which have enabled prisoners and university students to study alongside each other. Apart from the academic achievements and small graduation ceremonies to mark the end of these programmes, the most important educational achievement comes from two polarised social classes merging. It enables a breakdown of biases and false expectations from both groups of individuals who without such programmes would be unlikely to have ever met.

None of my interviewees had been involved in any of the prison to college programmes because they did not exist when they were serving their sentences, but when they applied to study at university following their prison sentences it was on the understanding that they would be afforded essential support. In most cases that was true, but some of them were treated quite shamefully by those whose job it was to help and support students. Debbie attempted to overcome the barriers of entering higher education by withholding her past, but her past came back to haunt her. After completing her degree she decided to enrol on a teacher training course, yet despite her proven commitment to study and the university where she had gained her degree, her past was scrutinised by a panel. She claims that it was as though she was being judged again for her past demeanours when all she wanted to do is move forward with her life:

> *I went and applied for my PGCE (Postgraduate Certificate in Education) and it's the hardest thing I've ever done but I stayed on and did that. When they found out about my criminal record for that and it was in the same university centre, that was a little bit tougher [...]. I had to get a letter from Sarah who is the CEO (of her current employment), explaining that I'd been here for four and a half years. It's my past and it's not a problem, Theresa had to write me a thing saying, 'she excelled at all'!*
>
> *(Debbie)*

There is no argument that for certain courses such as teaching whereby adults are coming into direct contact with children and vulnerable people, a full disclosure of one's criminal background is imperative. But perhaps the problem here is not so much about policy but about how individual cases such as Debbie's are handled by those making these judgements. Once the university eventually accepted Debbie's application, she successfully completed the PGCE and her case study has since been used as an aspiring example for other students. Perhaps though, the university panel should have considered how inspirational Debbie could be for other students before making her feel persecuted.

> *I felt very much like I'd been judged because of that. I got pulled into the office with the head and three people while they scrutinised me. I get it, if I was going to be working with vulnerable people; they needed to be sure who they were putting there.*
>
> *(Debbie)*

> *I felt like I was under the spotlight at that moment in time. Having to rationalise why, what and why I wanted to do... but they allowed me to (study the PGCE) and didn't find any fault. And after there was one day out of that year course, and it was over and done with and I was allowed to finish. They now use my files to show me round to everybody else so there you go.*
>
> *(Debbie)*

Although Debbie had to face some hurdles at university, she did not have to endure total rejection, which is what happened in Melody's case. Melody, a 44-year-old student at the time, had one of the most serious offending backgrounds, yet through studying in prison, she proved that she was serious about changing her life and thus began her self-transformation. Yet despite this, she was initially rejected by the first university of her choice:

> *I had done my 'A' Level. I had done my GCSEs in jail. Started the 'A' Levels, got released and my probation officer was really good, took me to college. Got 'A' Levels in psychology, sociology and law, which I thought would be enough to get me in and I was just classed, being twenty-five, as mature. Applied for a DIPSW and it was 'NO'! 'Someone with an extensive criminal record like yours will never, ever, get in any university in England or Wales'. I've still got the letter. I've put it away for when I do get the degree.*
>
> *(Melody)*

Aligning with anecdotal evidence from the Prisoners' Education Trust (2017), Melody's narrative highlights some of the discriminative practices by colleges and universities. This is also supported in Pike's (2014) study of prisoners who made attempts to enter college following a period of imprisonment. The university was more concerned about Melody's convictions than her academic abilities and achievements and she was therefore forced to regress towards a period of liminality (Healy, 2010, 2014). According to Ruby below, she believes that she was rejected from five universities because of her criminal record, although there is no evidence to support this. However, it is common for ex-offenders to make this assumption based on past experiences of stigma and rejection which understandably is what Ruby felt. Ruby, 40, was a substance abuse worker when I interviewed her in 2015 and has since gone on to become a probation officer. It was essential for Ruby to demonstrate her independence and gain a degree in criminology and sustain successful employment:

> *Got rejected from five universities because I've a criminal conviction. I applied for social work and the reason I applied for social work was purely financial, because the pay is amazing. (The first) University wanted to know more about my convictions, but they'd already lost my UCAS form so there was no way I was sending a DBS [background information of convictions] through the post to the university. I ended up with a proper snotty woman asking me my convictions, which clearly, I'm not going to share. Didn't get a place. The second university didn't even acknowledge my application.*
>
> *(Ruby)*

The common denominator between Melody and Ruby's examples of being rejected by universities is that they both applied to study social work which requires background checks for all applicants. Melody and Ruby then both successfully enrolled on to criminology degrees. This is why perhaps students with criminal records often veer towards studying criminology where a criminal background can be seen as a positive attribute. But if the lived experience is seen as being such a valuable attribute for criminology, why should they not be social workers? Surely having experienced the lived experience would give someone greater empathy and understanding which would be perfect for social work. A further irony is that although Ruby was rejected by the university admissions team to study a social services degree, as I mentioned earlier, she is now working as a probation officer. Prior to that role, she worked in a prison as a substance abuse mentor because of her lived experience. There seems to be spectacular hypocrisy here where it is not so much about the fact someone has a criminal record but more about how that information is managed by certain individuals. There are many examples of individuals with criminal records going on to work as probation officers such as Bob Turney (see Turney, 2012/2015) and social workers such as Allan Weaver (see Weaver, 2008; Weaver and Weaver, 2013). Weaver (2013) says himself,

> *I realize that I am in a fairly unique position in as much as I am currently a Criminal Justice Social Work Team Manager in Scotland and I am also an ex-offender and former prisoner.*
>
> *(p. 261)*

Using Weaver as a key study, Hylton (2014) goes on to argue:

> *...criminal justice and community rehabilitation professionals may agree that justice policy makers and rehabilitation professionals should take an interest in the views of those that have been on the other side of the supervision desk or prison cell door.*
>
> *(p. 287)*

These are well-known examples of how people with extensive offending backgrounds can make an invaluable contribution towards the criminal justice system. Yet when it came to some of the people in my study trying to enrol on courses that lead to such professions, they were met with hostility rather than encouragement. It seems that rather than offering any constructive guidance, some were immediately condemned such as in Melody's case where she was told that with her extensive criminal record she will 'never!' get in any university in England or Wales. I asked her how this affected her emotionally:

> *I went and got wrecked [drunk]. Inside? I felt 'f..k you!' I felt like going to rob someone, or shoot someone, you know? .... I would*

> *have probably hit someone before I burst into tears in them days. I've never been a crier. My anger would come out as violence instead of 'boo hoo'.*
>
> *(Melody)*

The people in my study and many other examples such as those mentioned above completely contradict what the admissions tutor told Melody. But she became angry and frustrated and as a result of being rejected drifted back into offending as her social bonds weakened (see Matza, 1969; also McNeill, 2012). One glaring issue here is that the professions are not always necessarily as in tune with universities as they should be. Melody's story includes a mixture of successes and unstable encounters more so than the rest of the sample. In addition to being told she would never be accepted into any university due to her extensive criminal history, this was made worse when shortly after she was rejected for a job application:

> *I applied for a job at the local drug alcohol service. I think I got down out of sixty people, got to the last eight but didn't get that. I thought 'bollocks to this'! 'I'm going back to crime!'*
>
> *(Melody)*

Ultimately, this led Melody to further consider full-time offending which is a common self-prophesying reaction to continual rejection, although there is no indication in either Melody's or Ruby's cases that they were unsuccessful in their job applications because of their criminal records.[4] In fact, considering Melody was shortlisted in the first instance would suggest her criminal record was not an immediate contributing factor because as we know applications are usually rejected at the first stage (see Unlock, 2018, in relation to 'Ban the Box'). However, continual rejections and such barriers that individuals encounter can have a significant impact on their self-esteem, and an important theme here is the language that is being used by others towards these vulnerable individuals. Individuals that work for organisations seem ill equipped to deal with people that have criminal convictions. Their responses are disrespectful, harmful, discriminative and unprofessional and not only lead to damaging a person's self-esteem but also create an internal label where they

4 Shadd Maruna and colleagues argue that there is a scepticism towards ex-offenders' claims to reformation might exacerbate the lack of success (i.e., produce high recidivism rates) by contributing to a self-fulfilling prophecy of sorts. If society is unwilling to take a chance on an individual who is trying to make an effort towards desistance, then these obstacles might lead to further recidivism. This, of course, is a central premise of labelling theory (Lemert, 1951; Becker, 1963).

begin (as with Melody) to self-prophecise (Maruna, 2012). But what happens when someone gets a criminal conviction while already studying at university? In 2004, Charlie (mentioned in the previous section) was rejected while he was an existing student and at the end of completing his degree. He was working towards a master's degree when it became public knowledge that he had been charged for an offence and as a consequence, the university where he was studying convinced him that he should quit:

> *I'd done enough to get my masters at the university [who] said basically, I had to resign. In some ways I had brought shame on myself and the university, so I wasn't awarded the masters.... I was either going to be expelled from the university.... or I had to resign, and my course director said: 'resign'!*
>
> *(Charlie)*

Charlie was shamed and removed from the university which was even more punitive than an applicant with convictions being rejected by a university. Some form of meeting and discussion would be an expected consequence of becoming convicted of a crime while being an existing student, but not only was he told to leave, he was additionally refused his master's degree which he said he had earned. But the ambiguity of all is that after being charged and later convicted, Charlie received more support from the prison than he had at university.

Sid, who was discussed earlier in Chapter 2, is a university lecturer who gained a degree in criminology and continued his education to doctoral level. He is active in prisoner and desistance research and has been instrumental in networking and the mentoring of other individuals who have left prison. Sid agrees that universities are changing:

> *At the end of the day [....] if five of us have gone for a job – me you and three other people – that haven't got a past like us, that are equally as qualified, publish the same papers got exactly the same things except for that tick on the box (stating a criminal record), it's easier I guess for them to go for that person, but they won't be as [pause] I don't think they will have our personalities David.*
>
> *(Sid)*

What Sid is describing is the increased cautious approach of risk when employing ex-offenders but Sid and I have both benefitted from working within universities. Therefore, to add yet another ambiguity into the mix, while we see universities as being punitive towards students with convictions, there are some who value the lived experience of their academic colleagues (including myself). Some recognise the advantage of the lived experience providing a new dynamic to teaching criminology and research but there is a confusing disparity amongst some universities on how they respond to staff and students with criminal convictions.

There are ambiguities where it would appear that while some universities embrace the persons lived experience, others see it as being shameful and therefore something they prefer not to be associated with. This ambivalence between prisons and universities offers alternative perspectives of the embedded dispositions that have always existed within both institutions. The pro-social approach towards education by some prisons contrast immensely to the history of violence and staff/prisoner power struggles within prisons (McDermott and King, 1988). Yet the libertarian ethos of education being paramount within some universities is being ignored when it comes to how they treat student applicants with convictions (Prisoners Education Trust, 2017).

3

THE PAINS OF DESISTANCE

One of the most important yet largely overlooked aspects of the desistance process is the emotional and psychological pain that is experienced. Other than Nugent and Schinkel's (2016) paper on the 'pains of desistance' which provides an interesting perspective that parallels Sykes' (1958) 'pains of imprisonment' there are no other studies specifically focussed on the trauma associated with desistance. Here I will argue that for some, desistance is more painful than prison because as discussed earlier, some individuals experience thought-provoking and positive moments in prison associated with early desistance. But once released from prison they endure many painful ongoing experiences, and whereas most prison sentences have a definite start and end date, desistance has neither. It can be very difficult to pinpoint when desistance begins as this can seem vague and I would argue for most, desistance is an unending sentence. Many desisters continue to experience deprivations of the self but also socio-economic deprivations long after release from prison as they attempt to reintegrate back into society. Therefore, the argument that prison can provoke positive transformations and that desistance involves ongoing painful experiences provides a contrasting and unique argument to that of previous desistance studies.

The previous chapter highlighted how imprisonment can create an existential crisis of the self which triggers individuals to self-reflect and reassess their lives. I have discussed how some are able to cultivate this towards self-improvement and identity transformation. So, it may seem quite ironic then that the desistance process in many instances begins to fall apart once these individuals are released from prison. The expectation would be that prison is the most damaging environment and that you rebuild your life once released back into society and yet in reality it can be the complete polar opposite.

Freedom often counteracts desistance as individuals become judged, rejected and stigmatised (see, Nugent and Schinkel, 2016).

THE VOID OF LIMINALITY

Liminality as a concept means a threshold; ambiguity or disorientation that occurs in the middle stage of rituals (rites of passage). It is when individuals no longer hold their previous status but have not yet begun the transition to the status they wish to move towards (see Van Gennep, 1960). While conducting my interviews, I did not specifically approach the subject of liminality in desistance because I was unaware that there was such a concept, but I knew exactly how it felt to be stuck in between the past and the present because of social stigma. I had learned this from my own frustrating experiences of constantly trying to prove my worth to employers. I could not understand how, despite having gained two degrees, I was still being shunned so in most cases I just did not apply for jobs that required a background check. I knew that I would be rejected so I remained stagnated for years after my release from prison in 1998. At the time, I felt as though I was the only person living this experience until I discovered the work of Dierdre Healy who coins the phrase 'liminal desistance' (2014). I then analysed the narratives of my interviewees through the lens of liminality and discovered (as I mentioned earlier) that liminality had been implicit throughout. Healy (2010) holds that

> *...liminal desisters formulate a clear vision of a desired future self but believe that a new identity, while achievable, cannot be attained in their current circumstances of liminality. In the meantime, the liminal desister develops a meaningful substitute self that permits expression of at least some elements of the desired future identity.* (p. 878)

This is particularly true in relation to the individuals in my study because most of them were working towards degrees, so although they had not quite reached the status they desired, higher education provided them with some of the elements of their future selves. For example, students by default remain in a stage of liminality until they graduate as a 'rite of passage' (see Van Gennep, 1960). But in terms of reaching for what most people take for granted such as employment, housing and social bonds, for those with criminal convictions, liminality becomes a prolonged and painful everyday existence (see Nugent and Schinkel, 2016). That said, it is also a necessary part of gradual progression throughout a life course. Nugent and Schinkel's (2016) study of long-term prisoners on licence refer to their liminal experience of desistance as the *pain of goal failure* whereby since leaving prison most had not been able to progress towards their desired identity.

The rite of passage (a term originally termed by Van Gennep (1960)) provides a good example of liminality that are devised or artfully created and are marked by elaborate rituals which commonly denote movement through the age cycle, marital status and social mobility. An example of a rite of passage is the university graduation ceremony which provides an official transition from student status to graduate. When it comes to desistance though, and as Maruna (2011) rightly argues, there is no formal rite of passage. This is in total contrast to the quite elaborate and rigid rite of passage within the criminal justice system starting from arrest to court trial and imprisonment. The Probation Service has always been a major influence in a person's rite of passage from leaving prison and helping with accommodation, employment and resettlement. However, we can see from some of the discussions in this section that experiences with the Probation Service did vary from one individual to another. Germaine, 29, encountered more obstacles than most which could be largely attributed to the media attention around her family's criminal activity. She is interested in the fashion and design industry which led to her gaining a degree, but during her studies she claims that despite her good intentions to move on with her life her goals were hindered by her probation officer who did little to help or encourage her aspirations:

> *I had bleeding probation with the claws in my back – useless. […] They were trying to meddle. 'What are you doing? Why are you going back to uni (university)? You need to come and do courses with us because you need to be rehabilitated!'*
>
> *(Germaine)*

Germaine then refers to her 'OASys' (Offender Assessment System) report which the probation and prison services across the country use for assessing the risks and needs of an offender.

> *I had to do my own 'OASys' report. They shoved me in a room and said, 'fill this in'. I just thought it was normal paperwork. I'd never been to probation before. Probation was useless. If anything, they held me back. Absolute nightmare! I'm sure it was because they didn't want me to go back to 'uni' (university). I felt like they didn't*

> *want me to progress. Whether it was full time, part time or just to do some kind of short twelve-week course.*
>
> *(Germaine)*

As we can see through Germain's narrative, her aspirations through higher education were being hindered by her probation officer who was more concerned about rehabilitative course work. This exposes some of the difficulties involved in making transformations while being both a university student and a probationer, and this was something I too struggled with. You feel you have partly moved on by becoming a university student, but at the same time you are constantly being dragged back by the probation service. They continually insist you comply to the rigid rules of form filling and attending meetings – along with the ever present threat of what will happen if you do not conform. But more than this it is the feeling of not being allowed to move on psychologically and being forced to remain in this void of liminality.

I refer to my own experience of attending weekly probation service workshops which were situated directly opposite the university where I was a student. Following each meeting which ended around 4p.m., I would leave the probation services building and head towards the school of social sciences or the university library to continue working on my dissertation. These meetings left me emotionally exhausted yet somehow cleansed, but the identity split of being a probationer/student created feelings that were intense, confusing and frustrating. While I was always praised by probation officers for my academic achievements and goals, they would continually remind me of my deviant profile and why I was on probation.

My experiences certainly mirror those of my interviewees because being a probationer and university student creates a significant 'divided self' (see Chapter 4, Bourdieu, 2004) which in turn creates conflict both internally and externally. And balancing these dual identities can cause a dislocation of one's sense of self whereby the past, present and future collide. Because of the emphasis on 'risk', the probation services can sometimes antagonise the situation by continually re-enforcing the ex-offender label through constantly reminding probationers of their past offending and what is expected of them (see Farrall and Calverley, 2006).

Germaine felt that even her own probation officer did not want her to progress when support and encouragement of leading a crime-free life should be paramount. Her probation officer had Germaine filling in forms and attending their 'rehabilitation' courses rather than attending (to their surprise) university. This is consistent with Pikes' (2014) study of ex-prisoners pursuing college programmes where she found that as with other organisations, the

Probation Trusts had obstructive and discriminatory policies and procedures. In Pike's study, this caused communication problems and at least one participant was recalled back to prison on a 'technicality'. Also, Farrall and Calverley (2006) found that while probationers were tackling problems relating to accommodation, family relationships and employment (all key to assisting desistance from crime), few probation officers appeared willing to engage in assisting probationers with their efforts in these matters. One of the most ambiguous cases in my study was that of Charlie who had worked with the Probation Services before his arrest, and admitted that he had a poor and judgemental attitude towards offenders:

> *If somebody was telling me about their drug use, I used to think 'oh this person is bull-shitting now – I bet it's a lot more than that'. Basically, I had already pigeon holed, judged somebody and probably written them off and gone in with loads of prejudices before interviewing them.*
>
> *(Charlie)*

Charlie's experience of imprisonment forced him to re-assess his attitude towards other offenders.

> *One thing that I would do differently now, I would, and I do think 'how would I feel?' because I have sat on that side of a desk where a professional is probably gone in with lots of prejudices towards me and thought, I'm lying and talking out of my back side […] So, I would like to feel that if I was in probation now, that I would be far more believing and understanding, empathetic and trusting.*
>
> *(Charlie)*

Perhaps Charlie's narrative and Germaine's experiences highlight a possible institutional and cultural problem within the modern Probation Services. That said, experiences with the Probation Services were mixed. For example, while Germaine felt they had never helped her, Melody said her probation officer helped her find a college place. Also, as mentioned earlier, Charlie's probation officer supported him and since my study, Ruby is now a probation officer herself. Jimmy, 47, on the other hand, had one of the worst experiences and recounts how he lost his education because of the actions of his probation officer:

> *I went along [to a university] for interview and did really, really well. So well in fact, that they let me straight on to second year […] I was liberated, I was attending university, I was doing pretty good. I*

> *was still on parole and I got recalled – that was a huge blow. It was a heavy hammer hitting, I'm going to lose all this work I've done, I felt that I was going to lose it I really did. I thought I'm half way through my degree and I felt I've f….d this up. It's self-recriminating. Fortunately, when I got back to prison there was no charges there was simple breach in parole conditions by some over-zealous parole officer [probation officer].*
>
> *(Jimmy)*

Jimmy explains in depth here how although he was doing well at university and was happy with his progress, an 'over-zealous' probation officer who like in Germaine's case, was absorbed about 'risk'. University was a transformative experience for Jimmy, but the probation service caused disruption.

Although for many individuals like Jimmy, education can have transformative benefits, it has limitations when it comes to certain groups of ex-prisoners. For example, Tom, 60, had served a 10-year prison sentence for sex offences towards his two daughters over many years. Therefore, the nature of his offences restricted his access to conventional university life, but he was able to enter higher education through the Open University (OU). For him, the OU was paramount because education enabled him to make a complete transformation. One of the major difficulties faced by many ex-prisoners is the struggle to find employment which can have a major impact on their sense of self but for someone in Tom's situation, there is a double stigmatisation (stigma) because of the nature of his offences (Milner, 2017; Hulley, 2016). Although, Tom achieved an enriched sense of self through education he feels it enabled him to question his life, and the behaviours of others also. He does accept his predicament with employment so has found a charitable organisation which has provided him with an opportunity to work while remaining in education:

> *It's not the prison because major firms have a sense of social responsibility; many of them, the Asda's and others employ ex-offenders – unless you're a sex-offender. My criminal conviction has prevented me from gaining any meaningful paid employment, and can create difficulties in relationships. I have, however, gained acceptance and unpaid charity work. I have also remarried and now live in a sheltered housing scheme in London. My educational achievements have transformed my identity, especially the way I view myself, and given me a sense of purpose.*
>
> *(Tom; Field notes, 2015)*

No matter what Tom set out to achieve, he was never going to be allowed to totally re-integrate. He would have limited academic access which means he would have to study through distance learning and would struggle with social mobility. This is not to say that the transitional processes that lead to desistance cannot be achieved by sex offenders (see Milner, 2017; Hulley, 2016), but rather it may take longer than it would for most ex-offenders and will require additional support. Hulley (2016) found in her study of sexual offenders and desistance, that desistance from sexual offending is argued to be a prolonged process, as the realisation of a non-offending prosocial identity occurs through the enactment of conventional roles. As seen in Tom's case, a sexual conviction presents additional barriers to attaining conventional roles, but Tom has achieved a graduate status through distance learning. He has married and has also managed to gain work within the voluntary sector and although Tom's convictions create added restrictions, most of the people in this study have, and will remain to have some barriers towards conventional roles because many convictions will remain 'unspent' (see Unlock, 2018).

Although the rite of passage concept signifies movement from one status passage to another, as we have seen, for the desister, this is often hindered through the actions of others including probation officers, employers and universities. The lack of support by some of the probation officers discussed in this study supports Maruna's (2011) point that the desistance process lacks anything representing a rite of passage. If we are to learn anything from this, it is that there are many examples in this study and beyond where desisters create their own life chances through employment, university, marriage and parenthood. And despite the often, undermining obstacles from organisations and individuals, they continually strive to overcome whatever barriers confront them.

THE PAINFUL NARRATIVE

It is evident from some of the interviewees' stories that the pains of desistance are more traumatic than the pains of imprisonment. But whereas deprivations within the prison setting are a consequence by the very nature of the institutional surroundings, the pains of desistance are not. They are created by individuals and organisations whose views on punishment towards people with convictions are in many ways even more punitive than the criminal justice system itself. But in this section, I will argue that these painful experiences can be a useful personal tool within the desistance process and that the 'painful narrative' enables personal growth. Nugent and Schinkel (2016) argue that desistance is generally presented in a positive light with themes such as 'making good', 'redemption' and 'generativity' (Maruna, 2001) and often associated with individuals who have long since desisted. This certainly resonates with my own study, but I argue that the desistance journey in my view should not be used in the past tense. This is because desistance is never-ending. Positive themes and generativity in desistance studies refers to Maruna's finding that desisters often work within roles such as counsellors as a form of redemption. Such roles involve a continuous dialogue between themselves and their clients whereby both actors are revisiting painful memories which can be an important process for personal growth. Therefore, I would argue, that we can synthesise such concepts as 'making good', 'redemption', 'generativity' and the 'pains of desistance'. And by doing so, create a broader understanding around the power of invoking painful aspects of the desistance narrative. Some of my interviewees have drawn extensively on memories of isolation, liminality and hopelessness to develop narratives of success and overcoming unsurmountable hurdles which have enabled them to achieve successful careers as mentors and counsellors. It became clear from my interviews that by drawing on these painful experiences this was an important part of shaping their identities. It was also clear that while reminiscing on some very painful memories this enabled the interviewees to make sense of some of what had happened in their lives and unlock many of their buried thoughts and feelings (i.e. 'these things happened for a reason').

Desisters have to continually try and overcome barriers and obstacles that may and do prevent them from reaching their goals, yet it is often through the most difficult experiences that they developed an unwavering resilience. Vaughan's (2007) 'internal narrative' highlights the ambiguity amongst varying narratives amongst desisters, some of who see the benefit of being reminded where they have come from while for others being made to revisit their past can be irritating. For example, Vaughan makes reference to a desister from Farrall and Calverley's (2006) study who is irritated being constantly reminded what he has done by his probation officer (as in Germaine and Jimmy's earlier examples). This is key because being constantly reminded about the bad things you have done is a far cry from being in control of what you choose to remember and draw from to self-improve. But it makes sense that both negative and positive narratives are encouraged when analysing self-stories, and we know that for many their desistance journeys started while in prison through a desire to change. With this in mind, it could therefore be argued that for some, experiencing anxieties and anguish was a pivotal moment towards their self-transformation (Giordano et al., 2002).

Judy, 41, had a lot of traumatic experiences throughout her life such as drug addiction and homelessness and at the time of my study was working as a mentor for homeless people. She was clearly distressed by her memories yet she painstakingly drew on them to explain what it was like. By doing this, she was able to articulate how these painful experiences enabled her to develop stronger resilience and determination. Judy became quite emotional when recalling a stranger's kind gesture that has stayed with her ever since. To many this would seem a small gesture but to Judy it was something that would stay with her forever. Judy was adamant about how important it is not ignore a homeless person, just showing some acknowledgement was the most important gesture one can make (field notes).

> *There was one occasion when a woman walked up to me, and I was sat at a bus stop miserable and the woman walked up to me and said are you homeless. I said yes and she pulled a tenner out of her purse and gave it to me. So, there's things like that – but overall a very shit experience.*
>
> *(Judy)*

Judy's painful narrative provides us with some insight into how she developed resilience through her determination to leave her environment and prove to others how she had changed. Dylan's painful narrative shines a spotlight on my earlier point about how the public view offenders and ex-offenders and how the publics attitude towards these individuals is often more punitive than the criminal justice system itself. Dylan, 27, already had a difficult start in life which had been influenced by his family's criminal lifestyle; however, he tried to escape this by going to university. This was almost cut short by the venomous reaction from his own peers after he disclosed his past during a seminar:

> *I declared I was an ex-offender. Leading up to this I was constantly spoken to by the rest of the course. Invited for cups of coffee. Then as soon as I declared that I was an ex-offender, I was instantly pushed to one side by the rest of the course… I stopped getting asked to go for cups of coffee. I stopped getting messages on Facebook from my fellow students and also, I was in lectures and they had obviously been 'Googling' my former crimes and laughing about it behind my back, whilst I was in lectures.*
>
> *(Dylan)*

Being shunned and outcast by his former friends was the last thing Dylan had expected, and talking about his experiences at university, he recounts the impact these negative experiences had on him. Dylan was in a difficult predicament when he was excluded by his peers which forced him to make the decision to re-take his first year at university, yet through this anxiety and anguish and a strengthening of resilience, he still managed to achieve his degree. His sense of self and personal identity was lost through this disconnection with others creating a sense of displacement and isolation (Nugent and Schinkel, 2016). Dylan recounted that these experiences reminded him of school:

> *I felt like that kid in school again. It really affected my confidence. The lecturers here have been absolutely brilliant. So, so supportive. I ended getting really depressed about it and had to repeat the first year. I just didn't say. I didn't want to make a fuss. Well I did say something actually, but I told them to get it off my chest. I've learnt now that it's good to talk about things isn't it, rather than bottle it up.*
>
> *(Dylan)*

This corresponds with Karen Graham's (2014) study of male prisoners' past school experiences. In her study, they reported experiencing the same feelings of isolation during imprisonment as they had felt when they were excluded from school. Graham's sample reported that as a result of being excluded from school, their friendships were tested because they were treated as being undeserving and therefore alienated from their peers:

> *What is common to the narratives is that the men were recognised as naughty kids, bad kids, kids with behavioural problems (and so on) at an early age, and these definitions seemed to be widely accepted by the majority of teaching staff, peers and the men themselves. These definitions or labels continued on from primary to secondary school, securing them reputations of tough or problem kids*
>
> *(Graham, 2014, p. 830).*

Being isolated impacted on Dylan's sense of self during his time at university as he becomes socially outcast by his peers and he felt displaced (see Nugent and Schinkel, 2016). An essential process of Dylan's desistance and self-transformation was that he had become reintegrated within the university culture but would now have to start again from the beginning.

As McNeill (2006) argues, sustained desistance improves when ex-offenders develop social links with people in different social hierarchies because it enables them to access wider social resources. Getting jobs, taking up new hobbies and being exposed to new experiences assist desisters in 'moving on' and building a new life, rather than merely existing in a stage of liminality (Healy, 2010; Laub and Sampson, 2003; Weaver, 2013). Although Dylan had tried to develop social links at university, they were then severed; however, rather than returning to criminal activity he continued with his education. As in many cases, Dylan could have so easily self-prophesied and returned to the familiar setting amongst criminal peers. Maruna (2012) reminds us that 'self-fulfilling prophecy is at the heart of labelling theory, so if others around us think we are dangerous and not to be trusted, we often become dangerous and untrustworthy' (p. 80). The self-fulfilling prophecy has been around many years now, but Dylan's account also highlights the possible vulnerabilities of divulging certain information. This brings me back to my earlier point of an under-explored area within desistance and biographical narratives of over-disclosing.

Because of the many positive aspects education can offer, one may find it strange to link education to pain, but sometimes knowledge can be a painful experience. The participants' experiences of education in relation to their self-transformation are varied. For example, some of those who had suffered domestic and sexual abuse as children felt that education added to their painful memories, which was one of the most alarming findings of this study. This linked directly to their suffering both in childhood and adulthood whereby knowledge gave them an insight into their own suffering (Frank, 1995). Some of the interviewees who were victims of abuse and domestic violence did not realise what they were subjected to was wrong, until they developed further insight through education. Although education provides further insight, it can be a negative, painful experience which, sociologically speaking, invoked an insight into the injustices they had experienced and suffered.

Len, 48, was the only life sentence prisoner in the sample and has not been able to completely transform because of the depth of trauma he has suffered. He came from an abusive, dysfunctional family life dominated by his patriarchal father where he was abused and beaten. Len found that education not only opened his eyes to the world around him. He became confused and more sensitised to his childhood traumas as he gained more insight and a realisation that he had been a victim of abuse. Len was asked if he found learning and education therapeutic:

> *No! the more I've learned, the more confused I've become [...]. Sociology is the subject that really screwed my head up, because all the life that I had accepted up to that point, hit me as being totally wrong. You know being beaten up by your dad – leather belt buckle and his steel toe cap boots, was all wrong. Up to that point it wasn't. I wanted to be like my dad. I wanted to be a friend of my dad.*
>
> *(Len)*

Education seems to have caused Len more psychological trauma which affected his relationship with his father, although he has explained that he does not blame his parents for his own wrongdoings. Jimmy found education to be both enlightening and at the same time a painful experience, claiming that education opens one's eyes to all the injustices in the world through gaining greater knowledge:

> *Bear in mind as well what education brings you. It brings enlightenment. You can see out of the box...when you become educated. In your dumb ignorance you just plod along in your own wee world. You do your own little thing. But when you became enlightened to the ways of the world and how things actually work and you see the corruption, you see the wrong doings by people of standing, people of note.*
>
> *(Jimmy)*

At times it is suggested that it is best to remain ignorant to what is happening in the world around us and that while education has opened doors and opportunities, it has also given them insight into an unfolding, unpleasant existence. Chloe said she had a confidence crisis during her second year at university because of not having dealt with personal issues:

> *I think I was thinking, I don't know why I am doing this [studying at university]. It's hard to get a balance between doing it because of your own experience. I just felt like I needed to get away from it. I don't think I had processed enough of my own stuff and perhaps it was still too close.*
>
> *(Chloe)*

Only Len, Jimmy and Chloe said they found learning to be a negative experience, but their powerful narratives do shed some light on an underexplored area within painful desistance experiences. Overall, the experience of learning and entering the higher education community was central to their positive transformations through the process of developing greater knowledge and being part of a new environment. The idea of formal education being a painful experience may seem surreal to many, as it is always presented in a positive light. But learning sociology, psychology or criminology involves delving into some very dark and traumatic subjects which can have an emotional impact on any student, let alone those with the lived experience.

4

SHARED NARRATIVES AND STORYTELLING

Analysing narratives is a way of interpreting storytelling so stories become an object of study, thereby focusing on how individuals or groups make sense of events and actions in their lives (see Riessman, 2005; Presser, 2009; Presser and Sandberg, 2015, 2019; Maruna, 2001). In this chapter, I will explore the self-stories and narratives of my interviewees and how their recollections of events and behaviours and imagined future selves (Giordano et al., 2002) became an essential tool towards self-change and identity transformation. As the interviews invoked past memories some of the interviewees tried to make sense of them like analysing dreams where they could remember a chain of events, but making sense of them was more challenging. Talking enables one to self-analyse and so the actual process of storytelling allows individuals to make sense of past experiences through a process of unravelling. While attempting to make sense of the past experiences, they also grappled with how they could move on to the next stage of their lives. Each was at different stages of their lives and some were experiencing more difficulties than others. Our narratives often resonated and as a former prisoner with similar experiences to my interviewees, I sometimes found this to be very challenging. Therefore, I will delve a little deeper into the challenges and tensions that are experienced by the insider/outsider identity felt by researchers who study groups of which they belong to or belonged to themselves. Also, as I discuss these stories in relation to desistance from crime, I will focus on the original and ground-breaking feature of this book which is of my personal experience and the process and subsequent immersion in the theory. In other words, as my study evolved I became situated within my study – a reflection of my own interviewees. Before my study, I believed that my own desistance journey had long ended because I had ceased to commit crimes many years ago. But as I learned more about desistance and the lives of my interviewees, I realised that I was in fact still desisting.

THE INSIDER/OUTSIDER DICHOTOMY AND THE 'DIVIDED SELF'

Throughout this book there is an underlying theme about the challenges associated with the insider/outsider position and the power of a reciprocal dialogue between myself and my interviewees. The insider/outsider dichotomy is the most unique aspect of this book where I become the protagonist of my own study which I began to realise as the interviews began to impact on my psychological well-being (see Honeywell, 2020). I use the term 'insider/outsider dichotomy' to refer to the tensions that exist when having two colliding identities during a research project. This was a consequence of being an ex-prisoner talking to other ex-prisoners who shared painful and sometimes nostalgic memories. It is an approach which can be borrowed from the discipline of existential sociology, where individuals relive their own experiences through shared narratives (see Kotarba and Fontana, 1984). It is also known as the looking glass self but what is barely discussed is how such research studies can impact on the researcher's own psychological well-being. And this is something that I had completely underestimated as an ex-prisoner delving into the personal lives of other ex-prisoners (see Honeywell, 2020). This links back to the section where I discuss 'the painful narrative' where discussing painful experiences are difficult and challenging but also important. And at times some of the interviewees channeled this by probing me about how I negotiate my past and present identities.

Equally in a curious role reversal of my researcher positionality, I began to probe those who had already reached academic positions I was at the time aspiring towards. Those who had already gained their PhDs and tenured academic positions gave me a blueprint of my imagined future self (see Giordano et al., 2002). This is part of the desistance journey which has nothing to do with criminality but rather re-inventing oneself, and it created a fascinating arbitrary dynamic. It made the interview process not just a negotiation of identities for the interviewees but myself also. From this time onwards, I was able to start developing my central argument about the desistance process being a seamless journey. My interviewees and I were all successful desisters in the sense we no longer led criminal lifestyles, but as identity transformation is central to the desistance process we were all still desisting. My research study became paradoxical as the stories of my interviewees connected with my own story which I had expected, but what I had not expected was the magnitude of how much this would impact on my own sense of self. I even began to feel I was part of my own sample and as a result, I developed a divided self (see Bourdieu, 2004). The divided self was a significant theme within this study. Because we were all attempting to develop new identities (Maruna, 2001), our past and present identities sometimes came into conflict. I feel it is important here to mention Pierre Bourdieu whose sociological theories seem a long way from those of desistance but his theory of the divided self is very relevant to the identity clashes that desisters experience. The divided self is the notion that individual biographies include dispositions (habitus) that translate throughout an individual's life cycle.

In *Sketch for a Self-Analysis* (2004) Bourdieu recounted that his own divided self was a consequence of the contradictions he experienced in coming from lowly social origins to achieve high scholarly distinction. And according to Friedman (2016), this seems entirely plausible because Bourdieu was from a generation that experienced similar kinds of social and cultural dislocation as a direct consequence of educational and occupational advancement. At times, reliving painful memories was as difficult for me as it was for the interviewees because our dialogue revived both our past experiences, but as I have already argued, revisiting painful experiences can be important. I would argue that the emotional connectedness and impact that interviews can have on the interviewer is as significant as any other data that emerge from research studies.

Also, it seems clear that if a researcher conducts a qualitative study with individuals who have many shared experiences with themselves, they will inevitably encounter the same emotions. Possessing both an insider and outsider identity, I was neither prepared for the unforeseen tensions created nor the intensity of these emotions and the impact they would have on my sense of self. Bourdieu's (2004) concept of the divided self provides an essential lens through which to conceptualise my own position as an insider/outsider. Prison ethnographic researchers have previously discussed the tensions of the insider/outsider position (Earle and Phillips, 2015; Davies, 2015), but because researchers are keen to complete their work, they continue regardless.

Lyng (1990) writes that much can be gained from retrospective reflexivity whereby the task is to make the research process itself the object of one's personal experience as a researcher. When these narratives are extracted from a researcher who shares the same lived experiences as their interviewees, it becomes autoethnographic. Ferrell (2014) coins autoethnography as 'the ethnographic exploration of the self' (as cited in Wakeman, 2014) which is still yet not accepted as a research method by some social scientists. Ellis also argues: 'Why does social science have to be written in a way that makes detailed lived experience secondary to abstraction and statistical data?' (as cited in Jewkes, 2011, p. 63). There would seem to be an underlying fear that if researchers disclose the emotions that have influenced their research that somehow the validity of their work will be questioned (Jewkes, 2011). Jewkes offers a strong argument that by not disclosing the emotional responses and autoethnographic roles within some very difficult and emotionally challenging environments such as prisons, they are 'doing a disservice to those who follow them who frequently approach the field with high levels of anxiety' (Jewkes, 2011, p. 64).

STIGMA AND THE SELF

Stigmatisation (Stigma) is an undercurrent theme throughout this book and although I haven't used the term extensively, it is something that is evident within every narrative. Stigma can be seen within the stages of liminality (Healy, 2010, 2014) and continuous labelling (Becker, 1963). Stigma is at every corner of the desistance process. It is the major obstacle that prevents desisters from continuing a smoother passage of self-change and transformation. The classic works by Erving Goffman such as *Presentations of Self in Everyday Life* (1959); *Total Institutions* (1961); *Stigma and Spoiled Identity* (1963) allow us to gain an insight into how destructive stigma can cause an indelible stain on a person's character. And throughout this book we can see how desisters try to overcome and outwit those who insist on staining their characters. In this section I discuss two of the female interviewees from my study who were particularly self-conscious about how visible their pasts were to others. In Stacey's case, it was the physical scars which were a constant reminder of the self-harm associated to the darkest periods of her life. For Chloe, it was her self-belief that others were able to just know that she had been in prison which led her to feel she had to explain her experiences to others.

Stacey's story is powerful and inspiring for younger people because at the age of 26, she was the youngest of the interviewees in the study who had already made great achievements. She had moved away from offending, her former associates and had transformed her identity through education and employment. With over 100 convictions, Stacey turned things around to become a postgraduate and youth offending service case manager where she worked with young offenders. Thinking back to her own youth, she argued that all her prison sentences were relatively short and wonders why she was never given a long-term prison sentence. Whatever the reason, there is no doubt this will have given her the chance to start afresh while still being very young. Later she was able to develop a student identity at an age where she was easily able to blend in with the majority of other undergraduate students and does in fact directly associate education to her successful desistance:

> *Education is my route out of crime. If I hadn't had gone to university, I'd have probably ended up serving a long public protection sentence, dead, or serving life.*
>
> *(Stacey)*

Stacey had worked hard to develop her new respectable identity; however, when she was invited to take part in a BBC documentary, the media insisted on portraying her as the stereotypical 'Ladette' (see Worrall, 2004). This had a negative and positive impact on Stacey's sense of self.

> *Obviously I did that BBC documentary. It's probably one of the worst decisions of my life, in the sense that I didn't enjoy it. I thought I was portrayed differently that I am. It was all true, but I always looked 'pissed off' in it. They told me to dress a certain way, and I'm not like that. I am quite a happy go lucky individual. They didn't want me to have my hair down, stuff like that.*
>
> *(Stacey)*

How Stacey presents herself is an ongoing and important process for her sense of self, so she clearly felt distraught at how the media presented her. The media created a spoiled identity (Goffman, 1963) for Stacey by portraying her as a poor, working-class individual with 'attitude'. For her young clients though it gave her more 'street cred' after they spotted her on the television. They made a mutual connection to the banter they had with her in the past which earned her even more respect. She already had a good working relationship with her clients because she was able to talk to them on the same level but until her media appearance, they had wrongly assumed she was a somewhat naive, white, middle-class student. There is a certain irony here because Stacey will have had a worse offending background than some of those young people she worked with who had made judgements about her based on her current identity, job role and appearance. Stacey was asked if her ex-offender status has become less important than it used to be:

> *Yes, I'm an ex-offender. I do go around on different talks and stuff as an ex-offender, but I always get across where I am at now. I don't want to be... you sort of prescribe the label of an ex-offender. What the hell is an ex-offender anyway? When do you become an ex-offender? You could go out and get a speeding ticket. Are you an offender? What do you call yourself? What do you identify yourself as?*

Stacey notes that she has prescribed to the ex-offender label and has delivered public talks about her past yet also emphasises where she is today so as not to be defined by her past. This is an important discourse which I have discussed at length in the following chapter where two identities become merged but then positioned within their own context. One aspect of Stacey's identity is invoked within a redemptive script (Maruna, 2001) which I expand upon in the following section. The other aspect of Stacey's identity is presented through what Goffman (1959) refers to as 'region analysis' where people choose which identity they wish to present in their front region.

No matter how much Stacey achieves, the past continues to linger, but the most important element of her transformation can be found within the fourth stage of Giordano et al.'s (2002) cognition study. This is where a person changes how they view themselves and no longer sees previous behaviours as positive, practical or even personally relevant. That is certainly a step in the right direction but to be able to move forwards, it's also important to the individual how others view them. Stacey was asked how she now views herself:

> *I feel horrible to admit, but a bit of me is a bit embarrassed about it. Especially meeting with people, meeting a partner. I am frightened that I would get judged for it and they would run a mile.*
>
> *(Stacey)*

This is an example of where the desistance becomes an extended, seamless experience. Although someone may have successfully completed a cycle of desistance, outside influences will still have a stake in how lives play out. For some, there is always that fear of being judged:

> *I do see people (i.e. dating) but I always have that gut feeling. I have scars on my arms for example. I never used to self-harm but in prison I lost the plot.*
>
> *(Stacey)*

Stacey is very self-conscious about her appearance and explains how important she feels it is to give the right impression even to the extent of hiding anything reminiscent of her past self:

> *[I] have scars on the tops of my legs and my arms. You can see they are not that bad, they're all old, small, but I have got a real thing about that. Even for work I never show my arms – ever! My close colleagues and my friends know, but they are like... 'Why are you even bothered?' It's weird, isn't it?*
>
> *(Stacey)*

Despite Stacey's complete self-transformation, she continues to negotiate the identity she wishes others to see. Her scars are a reminder of her darkest days which have an everlasting affect both psychologically and physically.

Chloe, 38, worked for a prison reform charity during the time of our interview and had gained degrees in health studies and social science and social research. She felt as though she used to over-disclose her past to others which also suggests a 'looking glass self' concept (see Maruna et al., 2004) where she felt it is important how others viewed her (as in Stacey's example). Again, this resonates with Goffman's (1959) 'region analysis' and the image Chloe wanted to portray to others – as someone who has paid her debt to society.

Chloe's self-consciousness about what others may be thinking about her impacted on every aspect of her life such as when she applied for a two-year college place:

> *...I probably over explained my situation, I don't anymore. I don't actually think it's anyone's business anymore. I don't do it in this job. I don't go to meetings and say, 'oh yes I'm ex-prisoner blah de blah'. It's not that I hide it from people. It's not like I'm ashamed. I just think that everybody's different. Like some people, they do*

> *that, and that's fine. I don't think that's a wrong thing. It's just something that I've learnt from my own experiences of doing that… that actually now I do this job now because I really enjoy it.*
>
> *(Chloe)*

There is no real explanation why Chloe felt the need to over-disclose her past to others, but this is something that people with convictions often do. Over-disclosing one's past is something some feel the need to do but it is under-researched. I briefly mentioned this in the introduction *examining the desistance narrative.* One explanation could be that because she felt her past was transparent to others, she somehow needed to put it into context. Maruna et al. (2004) argue that

> *…drawing on the symbolic interactionist notion of the 'looking-glass self-concept', the theory suggests that a stigmatised individual will come to view himself based upon what he believes other people think he is.*
>
> *(p. 274)*

Although this is gender specific, it can be related to both the male and female desisters:

> *I just felt like, I'd tell everybody because, I felt like everybody knew, like it was stamped on me and I would literally tell people [upset] probably inappropriately, over disclosing.*
>
> *(Chloe)*

Chloe's words, 'like it was stamped on me' is an interesting reference to how she felt she was labelled to the extent that others were instinctively aware of her past. It corresponds with Becker's (1963) labelling theory but I believe her feelings stemmed from shame and low self-esteem. She may have felt everyone could see through her but in reality, no one could actually know about her past by merely looking at her. Similarly, Stacey hides the scars on her arms as they remind her of her past self-harming, but also because she does not want others knowing about her past or making assumptions about her. The difference here of course is that while Chloe feels that her past from within is somehow transparent and visible to others, Stacey's scars are outwardly visible. Both Stacey and Chloe have now completely transformed their lives and reject their past identities which they feel serve no purpose to their current lives. The past can never fully disappear and will in essence always be the very thing that made these individuals what they are today. They are examples of two very strong women who have overcome unsurmountable obstacles to gain a good education and employment stability.

'WOUNDED HEALERS' AND THEIR REDEMPTIVE NARRATIVE

This section builds on Shadd Maruna's 'redemptive script' (2001) which consists of the evolving narrative individuals construct to integrate their pasts, present and perceived futures into personal identity. The movement of a redemptive narrative can be clearly seen from the different dialogues in this book and how some of the interviewees even interacted with my own shared lived experiences to try and compare with their imagined future self. In relation to desistance, Shadd Maruna developed his theory towards the notion of the 'wounded healer' (2001) whereby desisters attempt to make amends for their past wrongdoings through the work they do as counsellors and advisors. Similarly, Arthur Frank's (1995) 'wounded storyteller' about illness provides a narrative which can be translated to the struggles desisters experience within trauma, substance abuse, alcohol and relationships. Frank's work includes poignant accounts of ill people telling their stories in order to construct new maps and new perceptions of their relationships to the world. Some desisters experience illness as a result of mental health or/and substance abuse for example, therefore Maruna's and Franks ideas can be synthesised which support the benefits of ex-offenders working in mentoring roles such as counselling and drug and alcohol services.

In 2013, Kavanagh and Borrill highlighted how ex-offenders report strong feelings of turning their lives around by being in a professional position where they are respected amongst their peers and colleagues. Also how they felt they were accepted in the community and workplace as a professional worker instead of being perceived as an ex-offender. Maruna (2001) suggests that individuals feel that they should be able to contribute something meaningful to society, but that the 'redemptive self' concept is barely acknowledged within mainstream society. People with convictions should be allowed the chance to redeem themselves through employment, education and generally making amends. Gemma, 34, had been a habitual drug user and was stigmatised by her local community, yet later found work with the church and later as a senior substance abuse practitioner:

> *I started volunteering in church's drugs project [...] at the moment. It does all the food, homeless like a soup kitchen for the homeless.*

> *I started volunteering for them because I started thinking I wanted work in this field. As a lot of people do when they are in recovery and think I want to work in the drugs field. I say to a lot of them now go and try something else first because it is hard.*
>
> *(Gemma)*

Gemma said that lots of recovering addicts take up roles as drugs counsellors in order to help others as did Debbie who also found her work as a substance abuse counsellor very rewarding:

> *I have worked with people and I can see their journeys changing and it's the best thing ever [...]. You do it because it's rewarding genuinely helping people and you know you're making a difference [...]. It's not about the high salaries or... it's continuing to make sure that these centres stay open and that the women get the help. Even the men, get the help they need and get advice that they need. We do offer counselling. We're very much a one-stop-shop so there are therapeutic services here as well. The practical and the emotional side, they get that help.*
>
> *(Gemma)*

In a similar vein, Carla, 22, was working with one of the largest charities in the North East of England helping those who had drug and alcohol dependency with housing. In the past, Carla had issues with drugs and alcohol herself and drew on her experiences to enhance her work. As with Judy, Carla recognised that housing is essential towards recovery from substance abuse and one of the most important factors in reducing re-offending:

> *We deliver drug and alcohol contracts integrated with end of management. Housing – all sorts. We are a social enterprise.*
>
> *(Carla)*

Tariq, 28, was already a university student before being sent to prison which of course came to a sudden halt but at the time of my study, he had reconnected with university life and had since completed both an undergraduate and postgraduate degree. He explained that before going to prison he was a less motivated student than this time around where he found the whole university experience a positive one. Tariq was the only member of an ethnic minority in the sample which provided a useful albeit limited insight into some of the cultural differences for desisters (Calverley, 2013). During our interview, Tariq explained that he has aspirations to one day complete a PhD and currently continues with education and has been involved in local community police initiatives.

> *The thing is, in my job, I am working as a substance misuse family support worker. So, I have got a job in that kind of sector so it hasn't been that much of a barrier for me. It's only because I think because of the work I have put in. I have got two degrees. I have two work experiences, so people can see I work my socks off. They can see it was an isolated incident.*
>
> *(Tariq)*

Tariq was a one-off offender yet had committed a serious offence of violence and disorder for which he received a two-year prison sentence. However, he has worked hard to distance himself from his past and is now committed to working with families who experience substance and alcohol abuse and is even involved in a voluntary group at his local police station:

> *I work with families who are affected by substance misuse and alcohol abuse. So, I don't work with the person misusing substance or alcohol I work with their family. That's my main job and the other time I've got a second job. One of my dad's mates for a bit of extra cash. You'll find this interesting; I'm an independent advisory group at the local police station.*
>
> *(Tariq)*

Tariq had re-entered education as had some of the others which enabled him to transform his life. Yet despite Tariq's hard work and huge transformation, he still felt he had to do more to redeem himself:

> *I'm still trying to prove myself. I don't need to but I feel I have to. I feel I have to and now I've got my master's [degree] it does make me feel a lot better.*
>
> *(Tariq)*

Although Tariq could not be described as a persistent offender, he put his experiences of prison and the criminal justice system to good use. His strongest factor was that he had strong family support which may be why he has managed to make a smoother passage into employment than some of the others. Tariq is from a Pakistani family and though his family were all very supportive, their closely knit community were not always as forgiving:

> *When the incident occurred, people came around and they were quite sympathetic towards my family. No one ever said anything.*

> *They don't generally tend to say things to your face. It will be a case of later on they will be talking about so-and-so's son is in prison, did you hear about so-and-so's son, he did a bit of time. That carries a lot of weight in our culture because, not to say that shame isn't an issue in every culture, but it carries a lot of weight in our culture. It's really important and people attach a lot of value to it.*
>
> *(Tariq)*

Maruna found in his 2001 study that feelings of 'shame' can become a significant factor in the desistance process and as discussed earlier, it had a significant impact on Charlie and Len. It was also a significant factor in Tariq's desistance as he explains that convictions carry a lot of weight in the Pakistani culture because of the shame people attach to them and that redemption is an expectation and great emphasis is placed upon 'giving back'. Calverley's (2013) findings of Indian desisters correspond with what Tariq said in his interview as his culture being more focussed on 'giving back' to their close relatives such as their parents who had helped and shielded them. The strength of social bonds (Laub and Sampson, 1993, 2003) is apparent here, but Calverley argues that there is pressure on Indian families to uphold a level of respectability during the aftermath of their son's criminality. Although Tariq is Pakistani, there are similarities to Indian desisters in that it is usual to be afforded the support of their families which gives them a lot of love and support; however, this also comes with certain expectations. But Tariq does emphasise that although there are cultural similarities between Pakistani and Indian cultures, there are also differences.

The power of narrative has a significant part to play for those with the lived experience who work within generative occupations such as counselling/mentoring where they are able to use their positions to make amends as well as help others. But furthermore, I reiterate the strength of drawing on the painful narrative whereby working within generative professions could also be seen as a self-healing process (Frank, 1995). Healy and O'Donnell (2008) make an important observation that there is evidence to suggest that redemption scripts may not be as active in the early stages of desistance, and that the majority of desistance studies focus on past events which can be discoloured over time. This is a valid point, but the very process of engaging in conversation can be viewed as being part of the desistance process which coincides with what Presser and Sandberg (2015) posit: 'narrative criminology contests the popular notion that stories only rationalise past action. Bodly, it professes that stories also inspire action' (p. 287).

Narrative criminology is a fast-moving branch of criminology which has expanded quite significantly in recent years. In the *Emerald Handbook of Narrative Criminology*, Fleetwood et al. (2019) describe that although narrative criminology is only 10 years old, it is already moving in new directions. In particular, it has developed a greater understanding of human experience and meaning around violence amongst right-wing groups in Germany and how they justify violence through neutralisation; the narratives of serial killers of how they position themselves as having high morals; school shootings and personal recollections of being bullied; and other self-stories of mass violence, drug crime, alcohol addiction, cannabis growers and substance misuse recovery. Therefore, narrative criminology is fast expanding.

5

NEGOTIATING IDENTITIES

According to Maruna (2001) and Giordano et al. (2002), one of the most important stages of successful desistance is the process of casting off one's past offender identity through gradually developing a new identity that disassociates their present identities from their past identities. However, this chapter will argue that while this notion is pertinent to the majority of desisters, it does not apply to all desisters, which warrants essential analysis. In doing so, this chapter will discuss the narratives (Vaughan, 2007) of several desisters who self-identify as convict criminologists (ex-prisoners turned academics) and whose journeys of desistance in many ways contrast aspects of the desistance theory. The notion of separating one's past identity from their present identity does not fall within the convict criminologist's trajectory who presents an essential yet complex dynamic in relation to this desisting perspective. Convict criminologists maintain a dual identity which allows them to forge tenured academic careers (see Ross et al., 2010) as critical criminologists who make a myriad of contributions towards the advancement of knowledge in relation to punishment and the criminal justice system. However, to my knowledge, there are no studies using a convict criminologist sample in relation to their own desistance journeys conducted by a convict criminologist. In an almost chameleon way, some desisters have to continually change identities to blend in with new circles of friends, making a good impression to a new partner, their friends and families or submersing oneself within new communities, colleges or workplaces. Therefore, *Negotiating Identities* is a process that continues beyond abstinence from crime and criminality, so while the crime aspect of desistance remains in the distant past, the identity transition which plays a major role in desistance is fluid and continual.

DUAL IDENTITIES AND THE 'COLLATERAL CONSEQUENCES OF A CRIMINAL CONVICTION'

Although not discussing desistance specifically, Mobley (2003) stated very eloquently how only convict criminologists are able to transform their identities and sense of selves by merging both their past and present identities. Generally, the convict criminology trajectory through desistance is progressive because, essentially, the objective of the convict criminologist is to develop a successful academic career through which they provide critical perspectives on prisons and research with/on prisoners and former prisoners and develop a collective knowledge through their experiences and expertise to attempt to influence policy change through academic work and connections to advocacy/campaign groups (Aresti et al., 2012).

In a recent review of the past, present and future of the Convict Criminology organisation, Grant Tietjen (2019) highlights these complexities arguing:

> *...the pathway of a formerly incarcerated convict criminologist involves an ongoing process of attempting to overcome the stigma attached to the ex-convict label, and of grappling with the collateral consequences of a criminal conviction while also endeavouring to establish a legitimate and respected place within the academic environment.*
>
> *(p. 111).*

Mobley (2003) described this as the two-legged data dilemma (as cited in Jones et al., 2009, p. 159), meaning that

> *...symbolically, the ex-convict academic represents two antagonistic master statuses* the convict and the professor. *The former role informs the latter role but cannot be forgotten, especially when the subject of the research is prison.*
>
> *(Jones et al., 2009).*

And as Tietjen (2019) says, convict criminologists often undertake this process in the company of colleagues, who, while well intentioned, might not understand fully the unique structural hurdles in the pathway of the ex-convict.

Therefore, there is a difficulty for the convict criminologists becoming trapped within their own predicament of self-labelling, which can also create a split identity that can sometimes challenge one's sense of self. For example, holding on to the past can create tensions that relate to the 'imposter syndrome' (see Clance and Imes, 1978, see also Bourdieu, 2004) whereby the convict criminologists may question whether they could ever have become academics had they not exposed their past identities. In other words, merging two identities allows the convict criminologist to become socially mobile within the academy and develop a new dual identity, but on the other hand, the convict criminologist can become trapped within that identity.

We have seen how merging past and present identities is constructive for the convict criminologists in relation to their academic careers and how psychologically existing within two social worlds, which combine past criminal identities and current law-abiding identities, can be advantageous for sharing invaluable insight and knowledge. An additional argument in relation to the transformation of the convict criminologists' academic career is that the university admission process compels individuals with first-hand experiences of the criminal justice system towards criminology and cognate disciplines. The majority of the interviewees in this study felt compelled towards studying criminology and sociology because of some kind of calling where they felt that their life experiences could not only benefit others but also help them make sense of their own lives. But apart from their conscious decisions to gravitate towards these disciplines, it could be argued that the university admissions system also limits choices for people with convictions because of the rules around disclosure for certain courses such as teaching and medicine whereby background checks have to be made for all applicants.

This is not suggesting any form of discrimination but rather an impossible situation where no matter what progress individuals with convictions make, their educational and employment pathways will always be predetermined to some aspect. And thus, they become defined by their past lives in order for them to be socially mobile within academe, which as we have seen sometimes leads to a habitus clive (Bourdieu, 1977/1984). In other words, the extent of a successful criminology career for someone with criminal convictions may largely depend on using one's past to inform teaching and research, which further adds to the argument that the transformation is unending. Put simply, there can never be a complete transformation for these individuals who progress within academic circles because it is their misdemeanours that influence their success.

While some of my participants move further away from their former identities through education and employment, those who identify as convict criminologists choose not to and so they have to adhere to the constraints of the institutional habitus (Bourdieu, 1977/1984). In the same way as a person's habitus holds historical biographies that continue throughout life so do institutions. The institutional habitus (Bourdieu, 1977/1984) links back to my earlier discussion about the ambiguities of institutions as demonstrated by how some universities badly handle admissions from applicants with criminal convictions (see Prisoners Education Trust, 2017). However, there is also some contradiction to the institutional habitus concept which links to what I explained earlier in relation to employment. This is where some university departments (especially departments of social science and law) do offer individuals with criminal convictions opportunities to provide an essential contribution towards the advancement of criminological research and teaching. Therefore, there is an argument that while there is an institutional habitus that creates obstacles for university applicants with criminal convictions, in contrast, there is also an increasing amount of ex-prisoners/offenders teaching in universities (Jones et al., 2009). Discussing American convict criminologists, Jones et al. (2009) explain the development of convict criminology and increase of convict criminology academics:

> *Slowly, the (Convict Criminology) group has become stronger as ex-convicts have received jobs at academic institutions and risen through the ranks to get tenure, gain administrative experience, attract external funding, and complete significant research projects. At the very least, the past decade has proved that ex-convicts can be good academic citizens and make significant contributions to the academic literature while maintaining their original focus on prison reform.*
>
> *(Jones et al., 2009, p. 160).*

In the United Kingdom, Aresti and Darke (2016) explain that the British Convict Criminology Organisation (BCC) is growing and continues to recruit and mentor prisoners who are engaged in higher education, and like the United States, the network consists of a mixture of ex-con and non-con academics and has a healthy balance in terms of gender. Therefore, while the data in this study support the argument that university admissions procedures have been discriminative, it also demonstrates how the lived experiences of convict criminologists are embraced within some university departments. This is not to say that university admissions policies do not need to be revised, but rather that all universities need to be consistently fair in their treatment of people with convictions. The insight that individuals develop from their experiences within the criminal justice system that can then be passed on to benefit the academic world is captured here by American convict criminologists, Ross et al. (2010).

> *Numerous first-hand accounts of prison life have been written but until recently, accredited research from former prisoners equipped with higher degrees has been rare. After 1997 this began to change following the formation of a group of criminologists with experience*

> *of incarceration or of working with criminals in prisons. These scholars have begun producing research that is informed by their experiences of crime and the criminal justice process.*
>
> *(p. 2).*

In other words, convict criminologists have varying perspectives to offer as academics with first-hand experience of the criminal justice system and as academic researchers. I mentioned earlier that convict criminologists merge their identities through becoming successful academics while maintaining links to their former selves. This contradicts the secondary stage of the desistance process where desisters usually move towards developing a 'replacement self' (Giordano et al., 2002) and reject former identities (Maruna, 2001). It also contradicts Becker's (1963) labelling theory that individuals are treated as 'outsiders', which although is true for many people with convictions is contrasted by the convict criminologist profile. In fact, the interviewees in this study were using their ex-offender labels to progress aspects of their academic careers – though it must be noted – not wishing their academic success to be defined by their ex-offender identities (Jefferson, 2002). For convict criminologists, embracing both former and current identities become an essential disposition for their academic careers, but moreover, it becomes an essential process to overcome liminal stages and to settle inner conflict of their sense of self (Jones et al., 2009).

The crucial component to the success of convict criminology scholars is their rite of passage through higher education. Darke and Aresti (2016) argue that the 'transformative power of education and in particular, higher education has been documented in a growing body of academic work' (p. 28). They argue that the influential role of education and higher education plays a significant role in desistance which includes a complex interaction of individual, social and environmental processes and factors which involves a shift in one's sense of self and the emergence of a pro-social identity. Their claim supports the earlier discussion that there is a shift in one's sense of self which allows pro-social identities rather than developing 'a replacement self' (Giordano et al., 2002). Therefore, multiple identities can exist. Peter, 58 (also a convict criminologist), discusses below how sharing an ex-offender identity in education is essential:

> *Convict criminology is a way to build and share [...] experiences and the difficulties, you face. [...] Most people doing criminology have not been 'nicked'. They haven't been 'banged up' and they can write with a real insight and authority on it. But they shouldn't be*

the only people doing it. If there are people who can do that and work in [incorporate] that experience that you [myself] had and Sid and [anon] had into all those other training that you do as criminologists [...] that's why I think it's important to work with those experiences.

(Peter)

Peter feels it is important to share past experiences and through it develop new identities as criminologists that can offer a unique perspective for the benefit of higher education that other criminologists cannot. However, Ju Ju who was a psychologist and later imprisoned for seven years argues that holding on to the ex-offender/prisoner label for over a considerably lengthy period of time can eventually become a burden:

There's a time when the label gets too heavy and you've got to it put it down. There's no need anymore. I'm quite happy to support groups and talk about time inside with people like yourself because it's an important learning curve. But there's also a time in everybody life when they think, after twenty bloody years thinking, it's getting a bit old. There's new ground to break, so that's where I'm at.

(Ju Ju)

Ju Ju, 67, identifies where the ex-offender label can become tiring after many years of using it to define oneself but sees the importance of revisiting his past identity to support academic studies such as this one. Ju Ju is a white, English, middle class, heterosexual male who was sentenced to seven years imprisonment for statutory rape. He was British born but has resided in New Zealand most of his life. He was the oldest of the sample and has enjoyed a lifetime career as a psychologist and researcher. Education has been an important part of his life before and after prison which has enabled him to immediately overcome the barriers that others have encountered during their entry into university.

Sid was asked how the convict criminology perspective is important to his identity:

How could it not inform everything I do? How could it not inform everything ... the stuff that I lecture about? The stuff I write about? Everything I write about? The very fact that we've got British convict criminology [...] that old identity has to be part of it! It's like my old identity and my new identity have merged together. I guess what I am saying now [...] my identity now is a combination of some of the positive of the past experience and what I have achieved now and what I do now.

(*Sid*)

Here Sid explains how he has 'merged' his old and new identities which is the term Jones et al. (2009) use to explain the unique position of the convict criminologist (see p. 148). Sid views his successful academic identity as having been forged through a combination of past and present identities, as discussed above, that the criminology route was the most relevant given his past and that his new status of being a criminology lecturer (i.e., possessing a privileged knowledge) gives him a sense of identity that embraces his past and present identities:

Listen, it's a lot of things. It's certainly a protection thing definitely. It's part of my identity now. […] I'm not just any other lecturer right? 'doing criminology'. I am a lecturer doing criminology got f…..g experience that we are talking about. The prison stuff, the crime stuff this, that, and the other. So of course! If I was a lecturer in flower arranging for arguments sake, that identity would have no relevance, would it?

(*Sid*)

Sid who as we know is very open and honest about this past and has transformed his identity still continues to experience this 'visceral habitus' (Winlow and Hall, 2009, p. 3). Winlow and Hall (2009) describe this as being 'primarily defensive and cautionary', which can backfire when used as justification for impulsive and aggressive behaviour to perceived threats. They describe such 'embodied motivations' as a 'visceral habitus' at the centre of the subject's biographical narrative (Winlow and Hall, 2009). To put this into context, Sid sometimes experiences a divided self when his past and present identities collide, which can be analysed in Sid's narrative below:

The masculinity… yeah there is tensions sometimes. I did think, f…..g hell 'grow up you're an idiot!' when I'm in the car with my wife and kids and someone cuts me up and I'm off on one. And my wife's like, 'calm down, calm down there's children in the car!' Well actually I'm 47 years old, I shouldn't be behaving like that – like a f…..g 20-year-old but it's hard. People think, it's not only, it's psychological but it's also an emotional thing. If someone does something […] you just change automatically. Your whole f…..g body, just sort of … you tense up you get aggressive. It's an

> *automatic reaction and my therapist used to say what you need to do, when you're doing that in that situation, count to ten so you can think, so your emotions don't take over. It's a visceral [...].*
>
> *(Sid)*

Despite Sid's complete transformation of self, his new identity and successful career, he still has to sometimes deal with the challenges of his aggressive disposition. That is not to say that he is at risk of being violent, but Sid uses the term visceral which is instinctive or primitive and therefore something that is embedded within a person's self – a person's habitus (Bourdieu, 1977/1984).

THE ROLE OF BELIEF AND TRUST

In complete contrast to the experiences of discrimination, stigma and spoiled identities, many desisters refer to 'belief and trust' as having had a powerful effect on their self-transformations (see Rex, 1999). This was where they are strongly encouraged by others who believe in them that they can and will change. They also believe that they have something to offer and that they can also help others (McNeill et al., 2005). As mentioned earlier, how others view desisters is an essential aspect of the tertiary or third stage of desistance, but it is also particularly pertinent during the primary stages of desistance where there is always the possibility of lulls in and out of offending. According to Weaver and McNeill (2007), during the primary stage of desistance, it can take considerable time to internalise self-belief and therefore it is often a period of instability. Gerry, 36, was one of the most persistent offenders in the sample and had spent many years as a career criminal, mainly drug dealing. Yet after a lengthy criminal history, he began to try to make changes to his life. When Gerry was shown a little trust, it became a major 'turning point' in his transformation where he began to forge a new identity (Laub and Sampson, 2003). This is how he recalls the events around this period of this life:

> *I started volunteering with the Primary Care Trust (PCT) through another fantastic bloke called Ben who worked with PCT at the time. He took me under his wing – invited me to their offices. I remember the first time I went into their office, it was an open office [...] I was walking past desks and I past people where there were purses. There were wallets! there were handbags! mobiles and laptops! Thinking to myself, 'how the f..k is this guy trusting me*

> *with all this around me?' Just left me on a computer with all this around me! I think that was one of the biggest things. That trust someone put in me to sit next to a purse that wasn't mine and trusted me not to take it or touch it. I will always, always, remember that...always remember that. That was the biggest thing in my recovery... that someone gave me the trust.*
>
> *(Gerry)*

This symbolic gesture of trust becomes Gerry's catalyst for change – a major step that leads him towards his transformation. We know that for early desistance to begin, there needs to be an initial decision to change (Giordano et al., 2002), which can come from any amount of experiences. This was an important change in Gerry's transformation as it forced him to re-evaluate and question his identity. He began to evaluate how he had the opportunity to steal money while at the same time questioned why someone who knows of his past trusted him to be left alone in an office surrounded by unattended handbags and purses. This reflects the work by Rowe and Soppitt (2014) of desisters who reported that their commitment to desist from offending was rooted in the support that they received from staff with whom they had meaningful and sustained relationships of trust. This trust was developed through two programmes independent from the criminal justice system that they underwent and that was reported as a significant factor in gaining trust and confidence in their motivation to desist. This study has shown that the same trust and confidence can be developed between prisoners, ex-prisoners and practitioners within the criminal justice system.

Gerry becomes very emotional when recalling the trust that was shown to him and we begin to see an emerging pattern of how newly formed social interactions and social bonds through acceptance can influence the transformation of self:

> *Like within the drug treatment places you'd do your service user involvement thing and you'd be facilitating drugs, or you'd be pro-facilitating, but you were never allowed in the staff part. Now at PCT they allowed me in. As I say... gave me that trust and I felt really good. Every time I left that building I never touched anything. I wanted to succeed at that point. I wanted to get involved with that. I felt important, I never touched it. I felt good every time I left that building. Always had the thought, 'I'll just take twenty out, she won't notice', but never ever did. From that point on, I wouldn't say I never offended, but I never stole anything.*
>
> *(Gerry)*

Gerry was adamant that being trusted gave him the desire to turn his life around which ultimately was the catalyst towards his primary stage of desistance (Giordano et al., 2002). But typically during the primary stage of desistance, although Gerry had stopped stealing, he did not completely abstain from offending (Weaver and McNeill, 2007). This was because the trust that he had been shown linked directly to his workplace as opposed to his involvement with other types of offending. And although Gerry makes a very strong argument that the trust shown towards him was enough to stop him stealing, he still needed to believe in himself (Weaver and McNeill, 2007). We can see how Gerry starts to believe in himself as he begins to reassess how he views deviant behaviours. This is consistent with Giordano et al.'s (2002) fourth cognitive transformation stage of desistance, which is how the desister begins to change his/her views of deviant behaviour. Here he is able to show an understanding of how his mind viewed offending at that time of this life.

> *At that point in time I don't think I would know (whether to accept legitimate employment). I think for arguments sake if it was a thousand pound a week I was bringing home, I still think there would have been some form of offending. Whether that would have been dealing; whether it would have gone bigger where my funds could take me, within organisational crime or whatever, I don't know. I don't think any amount of money at that point would have stopped me offending.*
>
> *(Gerry)*

Gerry admits that he would never have accepted a legitimate job had there been an opportunity for one because a 'criminal status' was most important to him. But as we can see in his narrative above, he began to evolve within his workplace where he was able to hold down legitimate employment. Not only did this give him a legitimate source of financial stability but also a transformed sense of self and new identity. Giordano et al. (2002) view this as the the final stage of the desistance process because the desister no longer sees deviant behaviours as positive, viable or even personally relevant. Gerry began to 'cast off' (Maruna, 2016) his deviant identity that once defined who he was. He then aspired towards developing a renewed identity as a legitimate employee and work colleague (Giordano et al., 2002) within what McNeill (2016) describes as a 'moral community'. However, at this early stage of desistance, he still continued to drift in and out of crime (Matza, 1964) but became selective about the types of crimes. This could be argued as a form of desistance referred to earlier as a zig-zag process (Weaver and McNeill, 2007; Bilby et al., 2013). As time passed, Gerry began to progress up the employment ladder alongside entering higher education and eventually would make one of the most remarkable transformations of all the interviewees. This was because he was one of the most persistent offenders (see Maruna, 2001) and has continued to have one of the most stable lives. Earlier I mentioned that although employment, education and marriage and relationships can be significant turning points in successful desistance (Laub and Sampson, 2003; Shover, 1996), their significance depends on their stability. Gerry has to this day successfully managed to achieve each one.

Charlie on the other hand was unlike Gerry in that he was not a persistent offender (see Maruna, 2001), and therefore, it could be argued then that the process of desistance could not apply to him in the same way as it did for Gerry. Both were the same in that they desperately needed a break so when they were both confronted with the olive branch of belief and trust, this became their main catalyst for change. Charlie was euphoric when he was offered employment but still continued to internalise the shame (Maruna, 2001) he felt for his past offending and own the stigma he felt he deserved. Leibrich (1993) found shame to be a major factor in her participant's decisions to desist from crime but before Charlie was betrothed any trust, he experienced several difficult periods from day one of leaving prison:

> *When I came out of prison, I had to change doctors because my mum worked at a doctor's surgery. They asked me if I could change doctors just because she had been so traumatised by having her son in prison and all that. So I did and a doctor said: 'what do you want to do?' and I said, 'I might try and go into teaching one day or go back to social working' and he said, 'no you won't!' and that really hurt me and I thought – 'f..k you!' […] I made a determined effort that I would prove him wrong. My case went to the Department of Education and they said I could become a teacher if I wanted to, so I would like to think that if I ever want to go down the social work line, that they would have the attitude that this person could offer.*
> *(Charlie)*

Charlie internalised this derogatory comment from his doctor, which challenged his sense of identity, but he used it and other negative experiences as a pivot to overcome his inevitable anxieties. Such bigoted and discriminatory remarks may have had a greater impact on Charlie's sense of self considering it came from someone in a position of authority within a caring profession. But when the interviewees were able to utilise their negative experiences to strengthen their resilience and determination, their persistence finally resulted in positive experiences (McAdams, 2006). We can see this process when Charlie is offered employment:

> *I didn't think that I would succeed. Then I started volunteering for NACRO (National Association for the Rehabilitation of Offenders) in about January 2006 [...] then they offered me a job, and then I went home and was very emotional because I thought wow! Somebody believes in me. I can begin again. Then when the doctor said that sort of thing, I thought well I could go one of two ways I can either implode and be crushed by this or I can use it and fight and be determined.*
>
> *(Charlie)*

The negative comments from Charlie's doctor seemed to trigger a determination to succeed and prove himself, and the belief and trust afforded to both Gerry and Charlie ignited a passion to triumph. Through their own self-determination and through forging new alliances, they developed a new resilience which enabled them to overcome negative experiences and obstacles.

BELONGING TO A MORAL COMMUNITY

The higher education community provided the essence of identity transformation for some of the interviewees which was not just about education but also the social environment and new culture (see Laub and Sampson, 1993). Leaving one's surroundings is well-documented as being instrumental in desistance, and in the case of some of my interviewees, university campus offered this solution. University campuses also provided some with an escape from volatile environments that included many physical, emotional and social constraints. However, some were rejected the chance to take advantage of a new life and to live in university halls due to their convictions and so were forced to remain within the environment from which they were so desperate to escape:

> *They [university] got back in touch with me and said we need to interview you about your criminal record, 'could you send us a list?' I sent them a list, they had a meeting or something (amongst themselves) and said I am allowed to come to university, but I'm not allowed to use the student accommodation. I wasn't allowed to live in halls and stuff because of the violence on my record.*
>
> *(Dylan)*

Although the university accepted Dylan as a student, when it came to applying for accommodation, they requested a list of his convictions. This was so they could make an informed decision of his suitability to share accommodation with other students. This seems plausible given that there are safeguarding obligations for universities to follow, but policies seem to vary from one university to another. While some of those I interviewed were offered accommodation within the university campus (halls), others were refused. This is yet another disparity within universities which creates anxieties for people with convictions. Dylan's honesty once again backfired which sends out a worrying underlying message that honesty is perhaps not always the best policy. It could be regarded as discriminative, but universities see it as necessary to ensure the safety of other students. But one may ask how knowing of someone's convictions provides safety. Some would argue that a person with a criminal background is more likely to re-offend, but what evidence is there to support this? It is a prediction based on defining a person by their past mistakes. We could also ask who within universities are making these decisions and what knowledge they have of offending risk behaviour or even the person they are making decisions about.

Universities request that only 'unspent' convictions are required to be disclosed.[1] Therefore, students with 'spent' convictions can and are studying at university because legally they do not have to declare such convictions. The essential point here is that while universities are keen to weed out those with certain criminal convictions to decide on their eligibility to study at university, many students already have convictions and continue to enter university because of the 'spent' 'unspent' legislation (see Unlock, 2018). In Dylan's case, he had his own concerns about living in halls.

> *It (halls of residence) could be quite chaotic and I think they were afraid me being a bit older, maybe I would lash out. [...] I'm glad now, because in the first year I was living with eight, eighteen-year olds. It was absolutely mental! They were drinking every night. It wasn't the environment I wanted to be in. I could imagine the halls would be worse than the house I was living at.*
>
> *(Dylan)*

---

1 Convictions that are 'spent' as defined by the Rehabilitation of Offenders Act 1974 (as amended) – or will be spent at the point of taking up the offer of University – managed accommodation, do not need to be disclosed (i.e., not legally required to be disclosed). 'Unspent' convictions legally have to be declared at job interviews, for insurance claims and for some university courses (see Unlock, 2018).

Interestingly, the university regarded Dylan's past offending as a potential risk, but Dylan was concerned about the behaviours of the young freshers. As Dylan says, this turned out to be for the best, so while university bureaucracy may have thought it was protecting other students, as far Dylan was concerned, it was protecting him. Being on licence from prison or even just having a criminal record makes someone in Dylan's position very vulnerable. There would have always been the risk of him being caught up in something that may have ruined everything he had worked so hard for. But the real issue here is the universities' radical view towards people with convictions and their assumptions that they will be an automatic risk.

Yet in complete contrast, Judy was able to move into halls of residence which gave her the structure she needed. Judy also had a history of drug use as had Dylan but their offending was on a different scale. She found solace within the confines of the university where she was able to develop healthy social bonds with other students who helped her through her transformation:

> *The only people I had spent time with for years were other addicts. I was spending a lot of time with people in my halls [...] I very quickly assimilated into this new life. It was a revelation [...]. I wasn't being judged.*
>
> *(Judy)*

The words 'assimilate' and 'revelation' are key transformative terms that can be strongly associated with the desistance process. Because Judy was permitted to live on campus, she experienced a new environment in which she was able to adapt through her interactions with other students. They accepted her for who she was, which was in total contrast to Dylan's experience who was stigmatised by both the university accommodation services and also his fellow students (see Chapter 3). This supports how much social environment influences the desistance process which is not just about moving away from offending but also destructive lifestyles and the influence of certain individuals. Duguid and Pawson (1998) argue that for ex-prisoners entering university, particularly those integrated within campus life, the movement from prison to university provides them with another institutional identity and affiliation. It also provides an identity that substitutes the often derogatory labels. This is certainly the case for students like Judy where there is no doubt that university halls offer an essential bridge in addition to stability, security and total reintegration. But equally, there is no doubt that they are also potentially risky environments for those with criminal backgrounds.

Although some of the women in this sample found the college culture essential to their reintegration, for some it was much more than this. Moving to halls of residence was an escape from abusive and hostile relationships within the home. Before entering university, some of the female interviewees were offered accommodation within their Further Education College. This was an important turning point for them because during this period of their lives, they were experiencing domestic abuse and the college's acknowledgement of disadvantaged students in need of accommodation was tremendously important. It is common for universities to offer accommodation but not so much Further Education colleges, but for some of the women in this study, their own homes were unsuitable because they were victims of domestic violence. Clarissa was in an abusive relationship which was detrimental to her studies and unhealthy for her children:

> *I was in quite an abusive relationship with the father of my last two children. I tried detox; I tried community detox and both residential detoxes. Just didn't work for me at that time [...]. He used to hit me but at that time I thought I deserved that [...] because I was a heroin addict and he wasn't. Although he smoked weed and drank quite a bit at that time [...]. I was being sneaky and stuff like that you know. I used to nick money off him.*
>
> *(Clarissa)*

Clarissa believed that during the time she was using drugs she deserved the physical punishment inflicted upon her by her ex-partner. Fortunately, Clarissa eventually realised it was wrong and that she needed to escape her abusive environment which was not only an essential decision for the benefit of her educational progress but also for her safety and for the safety of her children.

> *Yes, you can live in. And you can take your kids with you and they see to the kids for the day [while studying] [...]. Honestly, it changed my life that place. It was great what happened. I started going to college [...]. I'd done methadone for years and years and I went on to Subutex. I started going up to [anon] College. Now [anon] College is a residential place and one of my key workers told me about it. I thought 'gives me a break from him and gets the kids out for a bit'. So, I just accessed little weekend courses and I loved it.*
>
> *(Clarissa)*

Eventually, Clarissa was able to completely break free of the abuse she was experiencing and give herself and her children the chance of a peaceful life. Gerry also found solace within the residential surrounds of the same college because changing environments for him was also essential but for different reasons. The need for Gerry to live in a different environment had been recognised many years earlier by his mother who changed his school to try and give him a chance to cut ties from his criminal associates:

> *I did my first course there (Anon College) – a drug awareness course. It was NCFE Level 3 Drug Awareness. Never been in education since painting and decorating, and this course work in painting and decorating. You're researching and writing essays and what have you. I just loved it. It's a residential college so it got me away from Leeds. It got me away from the immediate, all the risks of using and crime and from Leeds.*
>
> *(Gerry)*

For Gerry, being resident at his college offered him the chance to escape the environment linked with his criminal associates, and as with Judy, he began to mix with other people who had a passion for learning and seeking new beginnings. Gerry's transition was a complete metamorphosis from difficult environmental factors, drug taking, persistent offending and prison towards graduating from university and a continual upward social mobility.

Halkovic and Fine (2013) studied former prisoners in the United States who had all entered higher education. They set out to try and understand the motivations that drove them to enter education after prison, the obstacles they faced, the support that sustained them and the contributions that they brought to the university within their communities. They concluded that their interviewees were an inspiring group of marginalised 'others', suggesting that they had much to contribute to colleges and universities through knowledge, reflection, a sense of debt and a biography of transformation. These findings resonate with my earlier discussion about Maruna's (2001) 'redemptive script' where desisters often feel an obligation to give back. Halkovic and Fine (2013) suggest that although the cases in their study may be exceptional (i.e., each individual has overcome incredible obstacles to get into and through college), their stories are also diverse. This indicates that a wide range of people with varied backgrounds and criminal justice experiences have been successful in their transitions and have defined that success in their own terms. Ju Ju, who I mentioned earlier, is a good example of someone with a very diverse story which included working as a psychologist to serving time in prison for a very controversial offence (i.e., statutory rape). Yet he was able to continue as an academic once he was released from prison. Education has continued to be an important part of his life which has enabled him to overcome many barriers and help other people in his role as a psychologist and researcher.

Tom who I mentioned in Chapter 3 had also been convicted of sex offences, but as we know, he has not been able to make the same transitions as Ju Ju, but Tom did make exceptional progress in academe which boosted his self-esteem and gave him the confidence to confront his past. This could raise questions about how those convicted of sex offences are expected to reintegrate back into society. The difficulty here is that this subject is taboo and therefore many individuals could not even comprehend the idea of sex offenders and desistance or rehabilitation. Therefore, although education has not opened as many doors for Tom as it has for others, it has still impacted on his sense of self which was priority for him because of the anguish he had suffered as a child. He studied sociology, social policy and criminology through the Open University completing a first-class honours degree on release from prison. Since his release, and with additional support, he completed a master's degree in social research methods, and as Tom explains, education has completely transformed his sense of self:

> *Once I started achieving education, it challenged my thinking about […] I couldn't do anything, I was a worthless nothing. I was useless. All the self-esteem issues I had struggled with as a child growing up being told I was useless and couldn't achieve it […]. I was now in the small percentage academically of others in the country. I could achieve… and I can look at my graduation photos and I could go back home and say 'look what I did!' and that makes me proud. That totally transformed how I see myself.*
>
> *(Tom)*

Tom's transformation has included a combination of education, psychotherapy and self-reflection of his past life experiences where he was abused by his father which caused him deep seated trauma. Tom's narrative suggests that higher education had enriched his life to the extent that employment was a secondary concern for him. Moreover, it was about what education had done to improve his sense of self and most importantly, a change in his own attitude and view towards himself. The ironic twist in Tom's story is that he too was a victim of sexual abuse by his father and therefore cognitive changes became even more crucial. This sits within Giordano et al.'s (2002) third stage of their cognitive transformation theory whereby individuals see themselves in a different role as a 'replacement self' begins to emerge. Because Tom was convicted of a sexual offence, he assumed that his entry into academe would be limited if not impossible, which is why he studied online through the Open University. But Tom claims his decision to study through the Open University was not just about accessibility into conventional university but also because of the concept of Open University:

> *I actually love the concept of the Open University because I think it's the best value for money you will get. The materials are second to none. The resources they have available, the work they do with the BBC, the programs they produce and they are all over the world. I think are absolutely, they have superb materials. Most of the tutors are tutors at other universities anyway; they just do this as an extra. So, you get the best of all worlds – it's hard to discipline. It's hard to knuckle down and do it; it's hard to be very self-disciplined.*
>
> *(Tom)*

The links between the Open University and prisons have been ongoing since the 1970s, which demonstrates a strong historical understanding of the importance of prison education. This was recently captured in the first authoritative volume celebrating the last 50 years of the Open University providing higher education to those in prison (see Earle and Mehigan, 2019). It gives voice to ex-prisoners whose lives have been transformed by the education they received. Offering vivid personal testimonies, reflective vignettes and academic analysis of prison life and education in prison, the book marks the 50th anniversary of the Open University.

As noted earlier, some of the interviewees in this study were held in high regard by the prison education department and even entrusted with teaching/mentoring responsibilities. This demonstrates that in prison, possessing a good education can not only help to transform identities but also overcome physical boundaries within the prison education department. The prison education staff utilised the participant's educational skills which became transferrable for their futures. For example, we shall see in Clarissa's narrative further along that her university allowed her to able to deliver drug awareness sessions which had an important impact on her self-transformation and sense of self.

This is not the case for everyone though because some leave prison without the possibility of continuing the roles they adopted in the prison education department. While Tom was in prison, he was able to use his education to help others, but once released from prison, he lost his privileged status as an educator and at the time of writing has remained unemployable. As discussed earlier, this is largely because of his conviction being of sexual in nature but it also demonstrates the limitations of higher education and that it can only go so far in enabling individuals to transform their lives.

Clarissa, 41, had been a substance abuse user and eventually through education became involved in delivering workshops and seminars about her past experiences. She has also continued to work for the Council and has enjoyed delivering guest talks to college students about her previous struggle with substance abuse. Clarissa was a victim of child sexual abuse and later developed drug issues, but in later life, education provided her with opportunities not least including accommodation where she was able to escape a volatile relationship:

> *They (university) were ace! They used to have me in delivering sessions. They used to have me in delivering drug awareness sessions. I got a lot of confidence from that.*
>
> *(Clarissa)*

Clarissa's experience has had a positive impact on her self-confidence, and although this is very encouraging for others in the same predicament, it clearly highlights the inconsistencies of universities' treatment of ex-offenders. For some of the individuals in this study, education was more about changing how they viewed themselves, because until they were able to develop self-esteem, it was impossible for them to move on with their lives. Their past experiences had caused trauma to such an extent that this was a major hurdle but yet one that each and every one has accomplished in their own way. Tom and Clarissa had both overcome a history of being sexually abused which has left psychological scars but with very different outcomes. Tom went on to be sexual offender himself, but although this has become a barrier for him finding employment, he has found education to be transformative. Clarissa has continued to succeed through education and employment, and though her past experiences left an indelible mark on her, like the others it has made her a strong person.

(Clarissa and Gerry eventually married each other and have since developed a stable and loving home together with their children.)

6

CONCLUDING THOUGHTS

My interest in desistance (from crime) was born out of my own experiences which included making numerous unsuccessful attempts to re-integrate while being met by one barrier after another. I use the term re-integrate a lot but as someone once pointed out to me at a conference, who says we were ever integrated in the first place? That made me think a lot about the term re-integrate because it is assumed that those who broke the law left the fold and now want to return to it. It could be argued though that a lot of individuals, and I include myself in this, were never integrated in the first place and this adds to the many nuances of desistance theories. These nuances have been evoked by my personal experiences where insights are able to fill the theoretical gaps.

Since I began studying desistance theory, I have been able to apply its many components to my own lived experiences which have contextualised the many unanswered questions I had, in particular the notion of liminality (Healy, 2010, 2014). Reading the desistance literature and being welcomed into the Convict Criminology Organisation, not only made me realise I was not the only person who have experienced these things but also that it was not all because of my own doing. I had desisted from crime although I was never a career criminal and therefore in terms of desistance theory, I was not typical. I did have thoughts of criminality and a desire to be a criminal but by the time I had left prison, these ideas had begun to subside. The main obstacles I faced included social mobility and being able to have any career aspirations. We now live in a culture which requires background checks for almost everything and, though I can see the need for this, it can be very discriminative and wrongly managed by potential employers. The information that Disclosure Barring Service (DBS) checks give defines that person instantly.

VOICES OF THE LIVED EXPERIENCE

Throughout this book, I have reiterated that the narratives of those with first-hand experiences of the criminal justice system have in the past been silenced, but thankfully things are changing. Such accounts were only viewed as sources of entertainment through popular culture which included autobiographies and movies. In Chapter 2 I discussed the case studies of John McVicar and Jimmy Boyle, not least because of their influence on my own initial desistance because such biographies include important links to prison reform, education and academic research. These elements were clearly missed in favour of dramatising the famous prison escape that McVicar made in 1968 and Jimmy Boyle's ruthless gangster image. Both were difficult prisoners and rebellious against the prison system which portrayed them as unscrupulous, macho hard men who had no intention of following rules. But the media inadvertently highlighted the oppressive, toxic masculinity within prisons and a brutalising regime run by aggressive prison officers that existed in the day. It was something that would eventually lead the 1990s prison riots at Manchester prison [most famously] and others around the country. It was a time when prisons had to change, and following these riots, and the Woolf report, many outdated changes were made and for once prisoners' voices had been heard by the whole world albeit by force. Those who led the way in the riots were futher punished but changes have been made, yet there is still a long way to go for the voices of those who have the lived experience to be listened to without need for violence and destruction. It is not just the mainstream media and the public who needed to listen to these voices though but the discipline of criminology itself which for a long time favoured positivist approaches to humanistic approaches.

This is now changing but there is also a significant gap from researchers' reflexivity and even more so researchers with the lived experience. There have been attempts to bring existential sociology into mainstream sociology by writers such as Kotarba and Fontana (1984) and more recently to existential criminology (Crewe and Lippens, 2009) whereby accounts of researchers with various lived experiences are documented. Narrative Criminology provides this platform, but my own approach is quite nuanced because I have become situated within my own study and immersed within my own data but that is not unusual for a convict criminologist. Convict criminologists have begun to gain more recognition over the last two decades where they provide an essential yet complex position in relation to the desistance perspective, and influential narrative studies such as Maruna's 'making good' (2001) and Vaughan's (2007) 'internal narrative of desistance', to name a few, have helped bring the ex-prisoner narrative firmly under the academic spotlight.

The negotiating of identities is at the core of the internal desistance narrative (see Vaughan, 2007) which includes a complex, difficult and nuanced discourse. In the case of ex-offender scholars the difficulty for many is whether to remain stagnated between their past and present by hiding their past in which their upward social mobility may always be limited or whether to expose their past demeanors which potentially allows them to pursue academic careers as convict criminologists. Either way, both camps are limited because while for the convict criminologist, embracing both former and current identities includes upward social mobility towards tenured academic positions, there is a form of self-labelling. Being in this position can be translated to what Bourdieu described as a 'habitus clivé or 'divided self' – a splitting of identities whereby the past and present become interwined (Bourdieu, 2004). Yet merging one's past and present identities becomes an essential disposition for the convict criminologist's upward social mobility and academic career (Jones et al., 2009; Bourdieu, 2004). Several of the interviewees in my study were confused which direction to go with this so they attempted to gauge an imagined future self (Giordano et al., 2002) by asking me how I managed my ex-offender position.

The perspective of the convict criminologist is to make significant transformations both personally and professionally through merging past and present identities which enables ex-offenders turned academics to overcome stagnated periods of liminality but then remain in another liminal stage of dual identity. Desistance scholars argue that desisters begin to disassociate themselves from their former identities (Maruna, 2001), but for the convict criminologist, merging past identities with present identities is crucial for their upward social mobility as former prisoners turned academics (Jones et al., 2009). This therefore creates a continual process of self-transformation that links to their criminal past because the past identity for the convict criminologist has to remain attached to their developing academic identity and therefore the past always remains transparent.

Surprisingly, as far as I am aware, there are no desistance studies that have used a convict criminology sample and yet this is a group of individuals that by default challenge the very essence of desistance. They have made a myriad of contributions towards the advancement of knowledge in relation to punishment and the criminal justice system from tenured academic positions. They have not tried to or been expected to completely leave their past behind because it is their pasts that inform their present and future. Yet the desistance literature seems to have overlooked the major contribution convict criminology presents to its theory. This could be because they do not fall within the usual population of desisters. For example, they are few and far between and they do not follow the usual pathway of desistance which includes dissociating from past identities. In fact, their ability to manage and nurture dual identities through social mobility provides an interesting narrative. While other desisters struggle to cast off their past identities in order to develop new identities, convict criminologists choose to embrace their past which ironically enables them to escape liminal desistance (see Healy, 2010, 2014). Despite the essence of desistance being identity transformation, convict criminologists make this transition successfully by not disassociating from their past.

UTILISING PAINFUL EXPERIENCES

Maruna (2017) foresees the future of desistance being progressed by those with first-hand experience, and even within my PhD study the voices of those I interviewed and the reciprocal dialogue between us delves a little deeper than usual into the essential contribution those with the lived experience can offer. That is not to say that those with first-hand experiences of the criminal justice system know better than those who have not had these personal experiences but that their voices offer an important and additional dynamic. For example, the 'making good' narrative has become an important feature within these discussions, and desistance studies which highlight the value of the lived experience such as Maruna's Liverpool study support this. Maruna's sample claimed a higher purpose for their redemption – a reason to make good and 'fight the good fight' which many desisters go through working within generative roles as counsellors and advisors. Therefore, narrative is not just an essential methodological tool for research, but also a way desisters can make amends through a face-to-face'redemptive script' as 'wounded healers' (Maruna, 2001, p. 102). Desisters are well positioned for this kind of work because of their shared lived experiences of substance abuse which is why many choose to work in these professions. This resonates with Arthur Frank's (1995) book *The wounded storyteller* which is further discussed in Chapter 4 about personal accounts of health struggles with mental health issues, substance abuse and alcohol, all of which are common themes within desistance studies.

The wounded narrative replaces the 'criminal' identity for many desisters who do not view themselves as criminals anyway but rather people who have had substance abuse issues and later want to help others lead a healthier life. In Colman and Vander Laenen's (2012) study of recovering drug addicts, interviewees viewed themselves as drug users rather than criminals. This is additionally supported by Albertson et al.'s (2015) study of military veterans involved in drug use which shows that desistance involves much more than moving away from crime but rather a whole set of social interactions and transitions. For wounded healers, these interactions and transitions involve making amends through self-redemption while helping others to reform and improve their lives. Making amends allows one to present the 'real me' which becomes a powerful narrative throughout the desistance literature whereby individuals describe their renewed pro-social identities as the person they always were. This was such a dominant narrative in Maruna's study where his interviewees consistently referred to themselves as the 'real me' that he devoted a chapter titled 'the real me'. The real me is the person that always existed but was hidden by dysfunctional behaviours rooted within a life of crime and possibly substance abuse. Alisha Stevens refers to this in her paper *I am the person now I was always meant to be* which shines a spotlight on the narrative of one of her interviewees who used these words. Steven's explains: 'interviewees had created the necessary "cognitive shifts" to revise fundamentally the ways in which they identified themselves, and in so doing, had become less likely to revert to an "old" offending self and more likely to choose to retain the preferred "new me"' (p. 14). Maruna's 'Making Good' approach was influenced by the work of Dan McAdams (2006), where he employs narrative identity theory to explore the process of identity reconstruction through which repeat offenders reform and go on to lead social and productive lives. But it is not just the 'making good' narrative and the 'redemptive script' that is essential in transformation of self, but also the painful narrative according to McAdams (2006) who argues that life's lessons are learned through tragedy and painful experiences because they can ground certain individuals and change them for the better. He argues that painful experiences can bring people closer together where people often share profound memories of intimacy in their lives as times when they shared with others' deep sadness and pain.

Painful experiences are clearly as beneficial as positive experiences because they often lead to existential crises that force self-change. On this note, McAdams (2006) claims that the importance of the tragic narrative is a way of developing an understanding of self-transformations because anguish arises from knowing that you are alone and have to make decisions for yourself which becomes a powerful narrative in relation to existential crises and imprisonment. But equally, revisiting painful memories enable individuals to make sense of where they went wrong and how their bad experiences were meant to happen for them to find that real person (Maruna, 2001; Stevens, 2012). And as Nugent and Schinkel (2016) assert, it is just as important to draw on these painful experiences through narrative because as Stone (2016, p. 957) rightly argues, 'narrative theory of desistance is fundamentally one of "narrative repair" of spoiled or stigmatized identities'.

We have seen that sometimes prison can act as a catalyst for positive change and some individuals are able to nurture their experiences to make significant and often permanent life changes. However, whereas prison is already viewed as place of pain and suffering, desistance is rarely associated in this way but rather a period of redemption, making amends and reintegrating. However, Nugent and Schinkel's (2016) pains of desistance theory provides a useful conceptual framework through which to analyse this and the ongoing tensions that exist within the desistance process. Some of my interviewees demonstrated the importance of reliving their painful pasts for the benefit of this study but moreover, for the advancement of research. This perspective contradicts a lot of desistance related studies which tend to focus on the positive aspects of the desistance process, but this study postulates that for many, desistance is a lifetime process which can be painful and can include many tensions and personal challenges (Nugent and Schinkel, 2016). The painful narrative gives insight into how individuals use dialogue to make sense of their past experiences of isolation and hopelessness (Butėnaitė et al., 2016) and periods of liminality (Healy, 2010, 2014).

The theory of desistance has many flaws in that it overlooks some of its less obvious components (see Honeywell, 2019) such as liminality (see Healy, 2010, 2014) which is one of the most crucial and damaging aspects of desistance. Research studies can only draw on the information it receives but some of these less obvious aspects of desistance are even less obvious to those who are desisting. If you are unaware that something is happening to you, then how can you articulate that? Liminality is implicit in that is it not always obvious to desisters until much later in their desistance trajectories but even then it is difficult to explain. Long before I discovered the theory of desistance and in particular the notion of liminality or 'liminal desistance' (Healy, 2010, 2014), I lived for many years in a state of confusion. I existed within a void yet I was unable to explain it to anyone let alone find anyone who could remotely understand. And though it would be several years before I discovered desistance, the whole concept was still in its infancy and primarily focussed on external factors being paramount. Liminal desistance was unheard of until 2010.

McAdams (2006) argues that such painful experiences can help re-construct identities (Maruna, 2001) through understanding suffering as an essential part of human life and in this sense, some of the interviewees did feel it was important to revisit their pasts as a way of making sense of their journeys. The painful narrative is an essential aspect of narrative criminology (see Presser, 2009) that is perhaps overlooked in favour of more positive narratives because of the focus on successful desistance. But as we have seen through Maruna's (2001) 'wounded healer' and Frank's (1995) 'wounded storyteller' notions, revisiting painful narrative also enables a healing process in itself. But even when things can be made sense of or even put to rest, the constant barriers and stigmas that come with having a criminal record make a completion of desistance impossible. I reiterate, many desisters can and do easily move away from criminal behaviours but desistance includes a whole series of life changes and transitions that are continually interrupted and blocked by life events that cannot be prevented but in too many instances, through ignoranace and short-sightedness.

Research studies are limited to observing specific timelines consisting of a series of stages with a beginning and an end but in fact, desistance is often a seamless experience. As a former prisoner and desister, I am fully aware of the many turning points (Laub and Sampson, 1993) that aid desistance such as education, employment and relationships, but desister's trajectories continue to be an ongoing challenge which is more than often a never-ending experience. This book has gone some way to highlight the limitations of the desistance theories arguing that beyond the 'crime' related factors which desistance theory tends to fixate on, desistance is without end.

REFERENCES

Albertson, K., Irving, J. and Best, D. 2015. A social capital approach to assisting veterans through recovery and desistance transitions in civilian life, *The Howard Journal*, 54(4), 384–396.

Aresti, A. and Darke, S. 2016. Practicing convict criminology: lessons learned from British academic activism, *Critical Criminology*, 24, 533–547. doi: 10.1007/s10612-016-9327-6

Aresti, A. and Darke, S. 2015. Open prisons. An ex-prisoners perspective. *Prison Service Journal*, 217, 14–15.

Aresti, A., Eatough, V. and Brooks-Gordon, B. 2010. Doing time after time: an interpretative phenomenological analysis of reformed ex-prisoners' experiences of self-change, identity and career, *Psychology, Crime and Law*, 13(3), 169–190.

Aresti, A., Darke, S. and Earle, R. 2012. British convict criminology: developing critical insider perspectives on prison, *Inside Time*. Available at: https://westminsterresearch.westminster.ac.uk/item/8z319/british-convict-criminology-developing-critical-insider-perspectives-on-prison

Barry, M. 2015. On the cusp of recognition: using critical theory to promote desistance among young offenders, *Theoretical Criminology*, 20(1), 91–106.

Becker, H. 1963. *Outsiders*, New York, NY, Free Press.

Best, D. W., Ghufran, S., Day, E. and Loaring, J. 2008. Breaking the habit: a retrospective analysis of desistance factors among formerly problematic heroin users, *Drug and Alcohol Review*, 27(6), 619–624.

Bilby, C, Caulfield, L and Ridley, L. 2013. *Re-imagining Futures: Exploring Arts Interventions and the Process of Desistance*, London, The Arts Alliance. Available at: http://www.artsalliance.org.uk/sites/default/files/Reimagining_Futures_Research_Report_Final.pdf

Bourdieu, P. 1977/1984. *Outline of a Theory of Practice*, Cambridge, Cambridge University Press.

Bourdieu, P. 2004. *Sketch for a Self-Analysis*(translated by Richard Nice in 2008), Chicago, IL, The University of Chicago Press.

Boyle, J. 1977. *A Sense of Freedom*, London, Pan Books.

Burnett, R. and Maruna, S. 2004. So prison works, does it? The criminal careers of 130 men released from prison under home secretary, Michael Howard, *Howard Journal*, 33(4), 390–404.

Butėnaitė, J., Sondaitė, J., Mockus, A. and Romeris, M. 2016. Components of existential crisis: a theoretical analysis, *International Journal of Psychology*, 18, 9–27.

Calverley, A. 2013. *Cultures of Desistance: Rehabilitation, Reintegration and Ethnic Minorities*, London, Routledge.

Cambridge University. 2016. Learning Together: What happens when students from universities and prisons learn together? Available at: http://www.prc.crim.cam.ac.uk/directory/research-themes/learning-together [Accessed 24 May 2016].

Campbell, D. 2016. Glasgow gangster turned writer Jimmy Boyle: I would be dead now without books, *The Guardian*, 20 May [online]. Available at: https://www.theguardian.com/books/2016/may/20/glasgow-gangster-jimmy-boyle-prisons-a-sense-of-freedom-1977-republished [Accessed 24 July 2018].

Carlen, P. and Worrall, A. 2004. *Analysing Women's Imprisonment*, Cullompton; Devon; Portland, OR, Willan.

Cavadino, M., Dignan, J., Mair, G. and Bennett, J. 2020. *The Penal System: An Introduction*, 6th ed., London, SAGE Publications.

Clance, P. R. and Imes, S. 1978. The impostor phenomenon in high achieving women: dynamics and therapeutic intervention, *Psychotherapy: Theory, Research and Practice*, 15, 241–247.

Cohen, S. and Taylor, L. 1972/1981. *Psychological Survival: The Experience of Long-Term Imprisonment*, Harmondsworth, Pelican.

Colman, C. and Vander Laenen, F. 2012. Recovery came first: desistance versus recovery in the criminal careers of drug-using offenders, *Scientific World Journal*, 2012, 1–10.

Comfort, M. 2012. "It was basically college to us": Poverty, prison, and emerging adulthood. *Journal of Poverty*, 16(3), 308–322.

Cornish, D. and Clarke, R. 1986. Understanding crime displacement: an application of rational choice theory, *Criminology*, 25(4), 933–948.

Crewe, B. and Bennett, J. 2012. *The Prisoner*, London; New York, NY, Routledge.

Crewe, B. and Levins, A. 2019. The prison as a reinventive institution, *Theoretical Criminology*, 24(4), 568–589. doi:10.1177/1362480619841900

Crewe, D. and Lippens, R. 2009. *Existentialist Criminology*, Abingdon; New York, NY, Routledge-Cavendish.

Crewe, B. 2011. Depth, weight, tightness: revisiting the pains of imprisonment, *Punishment & Society*, 13(5), 509–529.

Cusson, M. and Pinsonneault, P. 1986. The decision to give up crime. In *The Reasoning Criminal*, Eds D. B. Cornish and R. V. Clarke, pp. 72–82, New York, NY, Springer-Verlag.

Darke, S. and Aresti, A. 2016. Connecting prisons and universities through higher education, *Prison Service Journal*, (225), 26–32.

Davies, W. 2015. Unique position: dual identities as prison researcher and ex-prisoner. In *The Palgrave Handbook of Prison Ethnography*, Eds R. Earle, D. Drake and J. Sloane, 2nd ed., pp. 463–478, Basingstoke, Palgrave Macmillan.

Duguid, S. and Pawson, R. 1998. Education, change, and transformation: the prison experience, *Evaluation Review*, 22(4), 470–495.

Durham University. 2014. *Durham University Launches Europe's First Prison Exchange Programme* [Online], Available at: https://www.dur.ac.uk/news/newsitem/?itemno=22565 [Accessed 25 May 2015].

Earle, R. and Mehigan, J. Eds 2019. *Degrees of Freedom Prison Education at the Open University*, Bristol, Policy Press.

Earle, R. and Phillips, C. 2015. Prison ethnography at the threshold of race, reflexivity and difference. In *The Palgrave Handbook of Prison Ethnography*, Eds R. Earle, D Drake and J Sloane, 2nd ed., pp. 23–251, Basingstoke, Palgrave Macmillan.

Farrall, S. and Calverley, A. 2006. *Understanding Desistance from Crime: Crime and Justice Series*, London, Open University Press.

Farrall, S. 2005. On the existential aspects of desistance from crime, *Symbolic Interaction*, 28(3), 367–386.

Fleetwood, J., Presser, L., Sandberg, S. and Ugelvik, T. Eds 2019. *The Emerald Handbook of Narrative Criminology*, Bingley, Emerald Publishing Limited.

Frank, A. W. 1995. *The Wounded Storyteller: Body, Illness and Ethics*, Chicago, IL, The University of Chicago Press.

Friedman, S. 2016. Habitus clivé and the emotional imprint of social mobility, *The Sociological Review*, 64(1), 129–147.

Giordano, P. C., Cernkovich, S. A. and Rudolph, J. L. 2002. Gender, crime, and desistance: toward a theory of cognitive transformation, *American Journal of Sociology*, 107(4), 990–1064.

Giordano, P. C., Longmore, M. A., Schroeder, R. D. and Seffrin, P. M. 2008. A life course perspective on spirituality and desistence from crime, *Criminology*, 46(1), 99–113.

Glueck, S. and Glueck, E. 1940. *Juvenile Delinquents Grown up*, New York, NY, Commonwealth Fund.

Goffman, E. 1959. *Presentations of the Self in Everyday Life*, 1st ed., New York, NY, Doubleday.

Goffman, E. 1961. *Asylums: Essays on the Social Situation of Mental Patients and Other Inmates*, Harmondsworth, Penguin.

Goffman, E. 1963. *Stigma and Social Identity. Stigma: Notes on the Management of Spoiled Identity*, Englewood Cliffs, NJ, Prentice-Hall.

Graham, K. 2014. Does school prepare men for prison? *City*, 18(6), 824–836.

Halkovic, A. and Fine, M. 2013. *Reentry Research in the First Person. Higher Education and Reentry. Education and Reentry: The Gifts They Bring*, New York, NY, John Clay College of Criminal Justice.

Healy, D. and O'Donnell, I. 2008. Calling time on crime: motivation, generativity and agency in Irish probationers, *Probation Journal*, 55(1), 25–38.

Healy, D. 2010. *The Dynamics of Desistance: Charting Pathways through Change*, London, Routledge.

Healy, D. 2014. Becoming a desister: exploring the role of agency, coping and imagination in the construction of a new self, *British Journal of Criminology*, 54(5), 873–891.

Honeywell, D. 2018. *Ex-Prisoners and the Transformation of Self through Higher Education*. PhD Thesis, University of York, York.

Honeywell, D. 2019a. Components of identity transformations within the desistance process. In *Strengths-based Approaches to Crime and Substance Use. From Drugs and Crime to Recovery and Desistance*, Eds D Best and C Colman, pp. 123–129, Milton, Routledge.

Honeywell, D. 2019b. Ex-prisoners and transformative power of education. In *Open University 50th Anniversary: Degrees of Freedom*, Eds R. Earle and J. Mehigan, pp. 195–218, Bristol; Chicago, IL, Policy Press.

Honeywell, D. 2020. The research experience from an insider perspective. In *Issues and Innovations in Custodial Settings Health Research*, Eds M. Maycock, R. Meek and J. Woodall, pp. 91–111, Cham, Palgrave Macmillan.

Hulley, J. 2016. "While this does not in any way excuse my conduct …": the role of treatment and neutralizations in desistance from sexual offending, *International Journal of Offender Therapy and Comparative Criminology*, 60(15), 1–15.

Hylton, J. 2014. Acknowledging desistance: a practitioner response to 'A view from the inside out', *Probation Journal*, 61(3), 286–291. doi:10.1177/0264550514547666

Jefferson, T. 2002. For a psychosocial criminology. In *Critical Criminology: Issues, Debates, Challenges*, Eds K. Carrington and R. Hogg, pp. 145–167, Devon, Willan.

Jewkes, Y. 2011. Autoethnography and emotion as intellectual resources: doing prison research differently, *Qualitative Inquiry*, 18(1), 63–75.

Jones, R. S., Ross, J. I., Richards, S. C. and Murphy, D. S. 2009. The first dime. A decade of convict criminology, *The Prison Journal*, 89(2), 151–171.

Kavanagh, L. and Borrill, J. 2013. Exploring the experiences of ex-offender mentors, *Probation Journal*, 60(4), 400–414.

Kazemian, L. 2020. *Positive Growth and Redemption in Prison: Finding Light behind Bars and beyond*(International Series on Desistance and Rehabilitation), Abingdon, Routledge.

Kotarba, J. A. and Fontana, A. 1984. *The Existential Self in Society*, Chicago, IL, University of Chicago Press.

Landesco, J. 1933. The life history of a member of the 42 gang, *Journal of Criminal Law and Criminology*, 23(6), 964–998.

Laub, J. and Sampson, R. 1993. Turning points in the life course: why change matters to the study of crime, *Criminology*, 31, 301–325.

Laub, J. H. and Sampson, R. J. 2003. *Shared Beginnings, Divergent Lives: Delinquent Boys to Age 70*, Cambridge, MA, Harvard University Press.

LeBel, T. P., Burnett, R., Maruna, S. and Bushway, S. 2008. The "chicken and egg" of subjective and social factors in desistance from crime, *European Journal of Criminology*, 5(2), 130–158.

Leibrich, J. 1993. *Straight to the Point: Angles on Giving up Crime*, Dunedin, University of Otago Press.

Lemert, E. 1951. *Social Pathology*, New York, NY, McGraw-Hill.

Lyng, S. H. 1990. Edgework: a social psychological analysis of voluntary risk-taking, *American Journal of Sociology*, 95(4), 851–886.

Maguire, M. and Raynor, P. 2006. How the resettlement of prisoners promotes desistance from crime: or does it? *Criminology and Criminal Justice*, 6(1), 19–38.

Maruna, S. and Farrall, S. 2004. Desistance from crime: a theoretical reformulation, *Kolner Zeitschrift fur Soziologie und Sozialpsychologie*, 43, 171–194.

Maruna, S., LeBel, T., Mitchell, N. and Naples, M. 2004. Pygmalion in the reintegration process: desistance from crime through the looking glass, *Psychology, Crime and Law*, 10(3), 271–281.

Maruna, S., Wilson, L. and Curran, K. 2006. Why god is often found behind bars: prison conversion and the crisis of self-narrative, *Research in Human Development*, 3, 161–184.

Maruna, S. 2001. *Making Good: How Ex-Convicts Reform and Rebuild Their Lives*, Washington, DC, American Psychological Association.

Maruna, S. 2011. Reentry as a rite of passage, *Punishment & Society*, 13(1), 3–28.

Maruna, S. 2012. Elements of successful desistance signaling. *Criminology and Public Policy*, 11, 73–86.

Maruna, S. 2016. Desistance and restorative justice: it's now or never, *Restorative Justice: International Journal*, 4(3), 289–301.

Maruna, S. 2017. Desistance as a social movement, *Irish Probation Journal*, 14, 5–20.

Matsueda, R. and Heimer, K. 1997. A symbolic interactionist theory of role transitions, role-commitments, and delinquency. In *Developmental Theories of*

Crime and Delinquency, Ed T. Thornberry, pp. 163–213, New Brunswick, NJ; London, Transaction Publishers.

Matza, D. 1964. *Delinquency & Drift*, New York, NY, Wiley.

Matza, D. 1969. *Becoming Deviant*, Englewood Cliffs, NJ, Prentice-Hall.

McAdams, D 2006. *The Redemptive Self: Stories Americans Live by*, New York, NY, Oxford University Press.

McDermott, K. and King, R. 1988. Mind games: where the action is in prisons, *British Journal of Criminology*, 28(3), 161–176.

McLean, R., Matra, D. and Holligan, C. 2017. Voices of quiet desistance in UK prisons: exploring emergence of new identities under desistance constraint, *The Howard Journal*, 56(4), 437–453.

McNeill, F. 2006. A desistance paradigm for offender management, *Criminology and Criminal Justice*, 6(1), 39–61.

McNeill, F, Batchelor, S. Burnett, R. and Knox, J. 2005. *21st Century Social Work. Reducing Re-offending: Key Practice Skills*, Edinburgh, The Scottish Executive.

McNeill, F. and Schinkel, M. 2016. Prisons and desistance. In *Handbook on Prisons*, Eds J. Bennett, B. Crewe and Y. Jewkes, pp. 607–621, Cullompton, Willan Publishing.

McNeill, F., Farrall, S., Lightowler, C. and Maruna, S. 2012. *Why People Stop Offending: Discovering Desistance*, Glasgow, Institute for Research and Innovation in Social Services.

McNeill, F. 2012. Four forms of 'offender' rehabilitation: towards an interdisciplinary perspective, *Legal and Criminological Psychology*, 17(1), 18–36.

McNeill, F. 2016. Desistance and criminal justice in Scotland. In *Crime, Justice and Society in Scotland*, Eds H. Croall, G. Mooney and M. Munro, pp. 200–216, London, Routledge.

McVicar, J. 1974. *McVicar by Himself*, London, Hutchinson.

McVicar, J. 2000. *McVicar by himself*, 3rd revised ed., London, Artnik.

Milner, R. 2017. *Desistance in Men Who Have Previously Committed Sexual Offences: An Exploration of the Early Processes*, York, University of York.

Mobley, A. 2003. Convict criminology: The two-legged data problem. In *Convict Criminology*, Eds J. I. Ross & S. C. Richards, pp. 209–226, Belmont, CA, Wadsworth.

Nugent, B. and Schinkel, M. 2016. The pains of desistance, *Criminology and Criminal Justice*, 16(5), 568–584.

Pike, A. 2014. *Prison-based Transformative Learning and its Role in Life after Release*. PhD thesis, Open University.

Presser, L. and Sandberg, S. Eds 2015. *Narrative Criminology: Understanding Stories of Crime*, New York, NY, New York University Press.

Presser, L. and Sandberg, S. 2019. Narrative criminology as critical criminology, *Critical Criminology*, 27(1), 131–143. Published online. doi:10.1007/s10612-019-09437-9

Presser, L. 2009. The narratives of offenders, *Theoretical Criminology*, 13, 177–200.

Prisoners Education Trust. 2017. Boxed In? Applying to uni with a criminal record [Online]. Available at: http://www.prisonerseducation.org.uk/news/applying-to-uni-with-a-criminal-record[Accessed 9 April 2018].

Rex, S. 1999. Desistance from offending: experiences of probation, *The Howard Journal of Criminal Justice*, 38(4), 366–383.

Riessman, C. K. 2005. Narrative analysis, In *Narrative, Memory & Everyday Life*, pp. 1–7, Huddersfield, University of Huddersfield.

Ross, J., Richards, S. C., Newbold, G., Jones, R., Lenza, M. and Murphy, D. 2010. Knocking on the ivory tower's door: the experience of ex-convicts, *Journal of Criminal Justice Education*, 21(3), 1–19.

Ross, J., Jones, R., Lenza, M. and Richards, S. 2016. Convict criminology and the struggle for inclusion, *Critical Criminology*, 24(4), 1–19.

Rowe, M. and Soppitt, S. 2014. 'Who you gonna call?' the role of trust and relationships in desistance from crime, *Probation Journal*, 61(4), 397–412.

Rutter, M. 1996. Transitions and turning points in developmental psychopathology: as applied to the age span between childhood and mid-adulthood, *Journal of Behavioral Development*, 19(3), 603–626.

Sampson, R. and Laub, J. 1993. *Crime in the Making: Pathways and Turning Points through Life*, Cambridge, MA, Harvard University Press.

Schinkel, M. 2015. Hook for change or shaky peg? Imprisonment, narratives and desistance, *European Journal of Probation*, 7(1), 5–20.

Scott, D. and Flynn, N. 2014. *Prisons and Punishment: The Essentials*, 2nd ed., London, SAGE Publications.

Scott, S. 2015. *Negotiating Identity: Symbolic Interactionist Approaches to Social Identity*, London, Polity.

Shammas, V. 2015. A prison without walls: alternative incarceration in the late age of social democracy, *Prison Service Journal*, 217, 3–9.

Shaw, C. 1931. *The Jack-Roller: A Delinquent Boy's Own Story*, Chicago, IL, The University of Chicago Press.

Shover, N. 1996. *Great Pretenders*, Oxford, Oxford University Press.

Stevens, A. 2012. 'I am the person now I was always meant to be': identity reconstruction and narrative reframing in therapeutic community prisons, *Criminology and Criminal Justice*, 12(5), 527–547. doi:10.1177/1748895811432958

Stone, R. 2016. Desistance and identity repair: redemption Narratives as resistance to stigma, *The British Journal of Criminology*, 56, 956–975.

Sutherland, E. 1937. *The Professional Thief*, Chicago, IL, Chicago University Press.

Sykes, G. M. and Matza, D. 1957. Techniques of Neutralisation: a theory of delinquency, *American Sociological Review*, 22(6), 664–670.

Sykes, G. 1958. *The Society of Captives: A Study of a Maximum-Security Prison*, Princeton, NJ, Princeton University Press.

Tietjen, G. 2019. Convict criminology: learning from the past, taking on the present, expanding to meet the future, *Critical Criminology*, 27(1), 1–14.

Tucker, J. 2009. An argument for offering higher education in prisons, *Academic affairs: Anthropology News*, 50(27), 27.

Turney, B. 2012/2015. *The Idiot Boy*, Hampshire, Waterside Press.

UCAS. 2018. Criminal conviction question removed from higher education applications [online]. Available at: https://www.ucas.com/corporate/news-and-key-documents/news/criminal-conviction-question-removed-higher-education-applications [Accessed 19 August 2018].

University of Westminster. 2018. Guidance for applicants with criminal convictions [online]. Available at: https://www.westminster.ac.uk/about-us/

our-university/corporate-information/policies-and-documents-a-z/guidance-for-applicants-with-criminal-convictions [Accessed 31 August].

Unlock. 2018. Ban the Box: removing the tick-box from application forms [Online]. Available at: https://www.unlock.org.uk/projects/employment-discrimination/ban-the-box [Accessed 17 April].

Van Gennep. 1960. *Rites of Passage*, Chicago, IL, University Press.

Vaughan, B. 2007. The internal narrative of desistance, *British Journal of Criminology*, 47, 390–404.

Wakeman, S. 2014. Fieldword, biography and emotion doing criminological autoethnography, *British Journal of Criminology*, 54(5), 705–721.

Ward, T., Rose, C. and Willi, G. M. 2012. Offender rehabilitation: good lives, desistance and risk reduction. In *Forensic Psychology: Crime, Justice, Law, and Interventions*, Eds G. Davies and A. Beech, 2nd ed., pp. 407–424, Chichester, John Wiley & Sons.

Weaver, B. and McNeill, F. 2007. *Giving up Crime: Directions for Policy, Scottish Consortium on Crime and Criminal Justice*, Edinburgh: The Scottish Centre for Crime & Criminal Justice. Available at: https://www.sccjr.ac.uk/publications/giving-up-crime-directions-for-policy/

Weaver, A. and Weaver, B. 2013. Autobiography, empirical research and critical theory in desistance: a view from the inside out, *Probation Journal*, 60(3), 259–277.

Weaver, A. 2008. *So You Think You Know Me?* Hampshire, Waterside Press.

Weaver, B. 2013. Desistance, reflexivity and relationality: a case study, *European Journal of Probation*, 5(3), 71–88. doi:10.1177/206622031300500306

Winlow, S. and Hall, S. 2009. Retaliate first: memory, humiliation and male violence, *Crime, Media, Culture*, 5(3), 285–304. doi:10.1177/1741659009349243

Worrall, A., 2004. Twisted sisters, ladettes, and the new penology: the social construction of violent girls. In *Girls' Violence: Myths and Realities*, Eds C. Alder and A. Worrall, pp. 41–61, Albany, NY, State University of New York Press.

INDEX

Printed in the United States
By Bookmasters